The Log Of H.M.A. R34: Journey To America And Back: With A Letter From Rudyard Kipling

E. M. Maitland

THE LOG OF H.M.A. R 34

JOURNEY TO AMERICA AND BACK

BY

AIR-COMMODORE E. M. MAITLAND
C.M.G., D.S.O., A.F.C., Royal Air Force

WITH A LETTER FROM RUDYARD KIPLING

ILLUSTRATED

HODDER AND STOUGHTON
LIMITED   LONDON

PRINTED IN GREAT BRITAIN BY
RICHARD CLAY & SONS, LIMITED,
BRUNSWICK ST., STAMFORD ST., S.E. 1,
AND BUNGAY, SUFFOLK.

Printing Statement:

Due to the very old age and scarcity of this book, many of the pages may be hard to read due to the blurring of the original text, possible missing pages, missing text, dark backgrounds and other issues beyond our control.

Because this is such an important and rare work, we believe it is best to reproduce this book regardless of its original condition.

Thank you for your understanding.

LIBRARY OF
CALIFORNIA

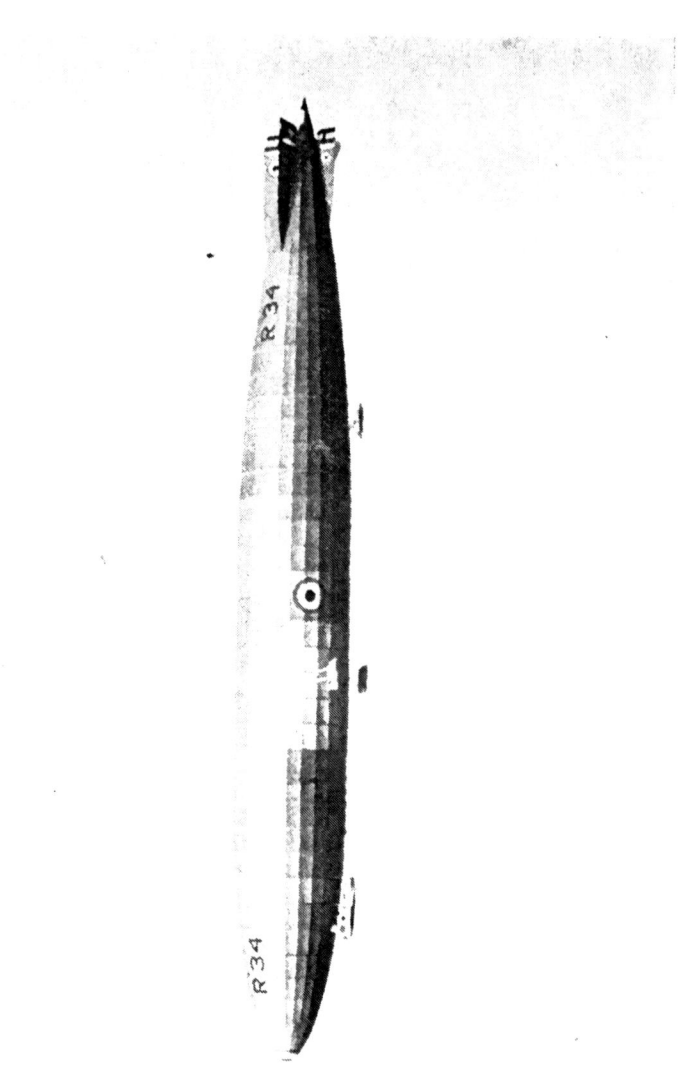

A LETTER FROM MR. RUDYARD KIPLING

Bateman's, Burwash,
Sussex,
November 26, 1920.

DEAR GENERAL MAITLAND,

Many thanks for your letter. I shall look out for R 34's log most keenly, and the more since, in my own mind, I always fancied the dirigible against the aeroplane for the overhead haulage of the years to come.

It's curious to think that R 34's work has been, relatively, no more than young James Watts' brooding over the kettle on his mother's hob. Watt, I expect, didn't realize the steam-loco (indeed, I believe he objected to it), but you, and every one aboard R 34, must have felt that you stood at the opening verse of an opening chapter of endless possibilities, and—I know what my own interest and pride were in seeing a dream shape itself and come true! There was not any one who was more earnestly and unbrokenly

PRINTED IN GREAT BRITAIN BY
RICHARD CLAY & SONS, LIMITED,
BRUNSWICK ST., STAMFORD ST., S.E. 1,
AND BUNGAY, SUFFOLK.

A LETTER FROM MR. RUDYARD KIPLING

*Bateman's, Burwash,
Sussex,
November* 26, 1920.

Dear General Maitland,

Many thanks for your letter. I shall look out for R 34's log most keenly, and the more since, in my own mind, I always fancied the dirigible against the aeroplane for the overhead haulage of the years to come.

It's curious to think that R 34's work has been, relatively, no more than young James Watts' brooding over the kettle on his mother's hob. Watt, I expect, didn't realize the steam-loco (indeed, I believe he objected to it), but you, and every one aboard R 34, must have felt that you stood at the opening verse of an opening chapter of endless possibilities, and—I know what my own interest and pride were in seeing a dream shape itself and come true! There was not any one who was more earnestly and unbrokenly interested while your voyage was under way; and if I had only known any saint who could have been trusted with the direction of our higher atmospheric interests at that time, I should have besieged him with offerings. So you see, in asking for my " blessing," as you put it, you have had it from the first.

Ever sincerely,
RUDYARD KIPLING.

INTRODUCTION

IT is often thought necessary to preface a first literary effort with apologies from the author for its shortcomings. In this instance no one could be more aware of such a necessity than myself. But am I entitled to make apologies? R 34 is not a literary effort—neither, therefore, am I an author.

In writing a story such as this, the obvious and comparatively simple course would have been the adoption of the conventional narrative form, helped by notes and memories, ample time and thought and a comfortable arm-chair.

Apart, however, from its practical usefulness or official importance, R 34's journey was just one long, wonderful and delightful experience.

To look upon this journey coldly as part of yesterday, or to treat it with recognized convention, would be to lose both the essence and the spirit.

My only hope of convincing my reader of this

is to try and induce him to share our adventure—taking him with us upon our flight.

Every word of this diary was written on board the Airship during the journey, with the exception of the explanatory footnotes and, of course, the appendices:—the writer perched in odd corners, and amid continuous interruptions and ever-changing surroundings, to the silent accompaniment of the wireless, like ghostly whispers across lonely space. Every incident, important or trifling, was recorded at the actual time of happening. Even to stop to focus or to pigeon-hole these would have been to destroy actuality.

If only I can share a little of that fascinating and buoyant adventure with any readers of these pages I shall be content. I only hope my ship-mates may not find their journey too dull; if they do they must not blame R 34, for the fault will be mine.

CONTENTS

	PAGE
LETTER FROM RUDYARD KIPLING	v
INTRODUCTION	vii
OUTWARD JOURNEY	1
OUR STAY IN AMERICA	87
HOMEWARD JOURNEY	95

APPENDICES

I.	CREW OF H.M.A. R 34	133
II.	H.M.A. R 34—WATCH AND STATION BILL .	135
III.	FOOD SUPPLIES FOR OUTWARD AND HOMEWARD JOURNEYS	140
IV.	NAVIGATIONAL INSTRUMENTS AND BOOKS .	142
V.	WIRELESS LOG OF H.M.A. R 34 . . .	143
VI.	HANDLING SHIP DURING THE NIGHT: AEROSTATIC CONDITIONS	167
VII.	CHART OF ATLANTIC, SHOWING TRACK OF OUTWARD AND HOMEWARD JOURNEYS: ALSO METEOROLOGICAL AND WIRELESS TELEGRAPHY STATIONS	169

ILLUSTRATIONS

To face page

R 34 *(Copyright Photo)* . . . . *Frontispiece*

MAJOR SCOTT, BEFORE SOLUTION OF THE PROBLEM . 16

MAJOR SCOTT, AFTER SOLUTION OF THE PROBLEM . 16

CONTROL CAR—FLIGHT-SERGT. WATSON STEERING. FLIGHT-SERGT. MAYES AT THE ELEVATOR WHEEL 22

CREW SPACE INSIDE HULL 22

SHADOW OF R 34 THROWN UPON A LOW BANK OF CURIOUSLY BANDED CLOUDS 26

SERIES OF FIVE PHOTOGRAPHS SHOWING THE PASSAGE OF A CYCLONE—

    R 34 FLYING JUST ABOVE DENSE CLOUDS ON THE OUTSKIRTS OF A DEPRESSION . . 28

    SUNSET—STILL ABOVE THE CLOUDS AND NEARING CENTRE OF DEPRESSION 30

    ABOVE THE WORST OF THE DEPRESSION SOON AFTER SUNSET 30

    FIRST GLIMPSE OF ATLANTIC AFTER PASSAGE OF CYCLONE 32

    NEXT MORNING. THE CALM AFTER THE STORM. 32

DESOLATE COUNTRY IN THE INTERIOR OF NEWFOUNDLAND 64

R 34 OVER THE TOWN OF FORTUNE 64

ILLUSTRATIONS

To face page

First Sight of Long Island	80
The First Man to arrive in America by way of the Air	80
A Group of some of the Officers after Landing in America	89
R 34 moored out at Mineola, viewed by Searchlight	89
Cloud Shadows thrown upon the Atlantic .	104
Interior of R 34 showing Walking-way and Petrol Tanks	104
Low-lying Cumulus Clouds	126
Above the Hills and Lakes of North Ireland .	126
Hauling on the Trail Rope. The End of the Journey	128
Preparing to Land at H.M. Airship Station, Pulham, Norfolk	128
Group of Officers taken after Landing . .	133

OUTWARD JOURNEY

WEDNESDAY, JULY 2ND, 1919

MIDNIGHT on a wet and windy night in July, and the big Airship Station at East Fortune is all agog with bustle and excitement.

The moment eagerly anticipated for weeks past has at last arrived, and R 34—Britain's largest and most efficient Rigid Airship—is about to start upon her 3000 miles' journey across the Atlantic, bound for Long Island—New York.

In the ordinary course of events the Airship Station at this hour would be peacefully asleep; but now there are lights everywhere, orders are sharply given and promptly obeyed, and final arrangements hurriedly carried out.

At 1 a.m. the crew of eight officers and twenty-two men climb aboard, dressed in their flying clothes, having had an excellent dinner to fortify them for their long journey.

The ship is now quite ready; stocks of food have been taken on board—sleeping equipment, and, indeed, the thousand-and-one preparations incidental to an enterprise of this kind, have all been completed.

Amongst a host of other things, we have on board valuable films of the Peace Conference, a consignment of platinum for a firm of New York jewellers, and English newspapers for the editors of the *New York Times* and *Public Ledger.*

Weather Conditions.—At first sight the weather looks far from suitable. It is very dark—rain is falling slightly—the clouds appear to be very low, and the wind whistles mournfully round the corner of the big Airship shed.

The weather reports, however, in mid-Atlantic are more or less favourable. There is a depression in the North Sea centred east of Flamboro' Head, moving slowly southward, an anti-cyclone covers the greater part of the North Atlantic, another is reported over the great lakes of Canada, whilst unusual quiet exists over the whole of the North Atlantic Ocean. The wind in the West of Scotland and North of Ireland is from the north-east, and may prove of assistance to us until we are well out into the Atlantic.

Major Scott, therefore, decides, despite the bad local weather conditions, to get away as soon as possible.

Objects of the Voyage.—The Air Ministry have

several definite objectives in sending R 34 upon this flight.

Firstly, the acquisition of information and data concerning conditions in the Atlantic during an extended flight : not only from the point of view of the Airship pilot, but also from the point of view of the Meteorologist.

Secondly, to demonstrate the possibilities of large Rigid Airships with regard to carrying out long oversea voyages; and finally, by actually landing in the United States of America, to show our friends across the Atlantic our newest type of Airship, and at the same time to forge a new link, by way of the air, between the Old World and the New.

What more wonderful or more delightful adventure could any one be called upon to undertake?

We one and all have the greatest confidence both in our Captain and in our Airship, and it is never a question of " *Are* we going to get to America? " but " How long will it take us to get to America? "

Time, 1.23 *a.m.* (Greenwich mean time).[1]— Everything is now ready. The bugle sounds,

[1] All times given are Greenwich mean time except where otherwise stated.

and the handling party commence walking the ship slowly out of the shed stern first.

The wind is blowing from the north east, and the ship is facing S.W. as she is walked out.

1.30 *a.m.*—Ship is swung round facing into the wind as soon as her stern is clear of the wind screens.

1.37 *a.m.*—Ballasting up. Gas-bags 99 per cent. full.

1.39 *a.m.*—Engines started up.

1.42 *a.m.*—At a signal from Scott, the bugle sounds the "Let go," the huge Airship slowly rises from the hands of the handling party, and is immediately swallowed up in the low-lying clouds at a height of 100 feet.

Rousing cheers reach us through the clouds, and hearten us for the task we have in front of us.

When flying at night, possibly on account of the darkness, there is always a feeling of utter loneliness directly one loses sight of the ground. We feel this loneliness very much to-night; possibly owing to the fact that we are bound for a totally unknown destination across the wide Atlantic. Such a feeling is only momentary, however, and is soon dispelled by the immediate need for action. Scott rings down 600 revolu-

OUTWARD JOURNEY

tions on all five engines, and each engine-room in turn acknowledges the signal on the dial in the foremost car.

Cooke, our navigator, sets a course N.W. for Rosyth and the Clyde.

Scott takes his ship up to the 1500-foot level, and lets go a quarter of a ton of water ballast so as to clear all sheds and other obstacles, the ship getting away about one ton heavy.

1.49 *a.m.*—1600 revolutions on all five engines, speed forty-five knots, height 1000 feet. We are now almost above the clouds, with here and there a gap through which an occasional light on the ground can be seen. Course steered 225°. Course making good 287° N.W.

2 *a.m.*—1500 feet. Completely above clouds. Inky darkness.

Great satisfaction in getting away on scheduled time. A week previously it had been announced that R 34 would leave for U.S.A. at 2 a.m. on Wednesday, July 2nd, therefore she actually commenced her journey a few minutes before scheduled time.

2.5 *a.m.*—In clouds again—1500 feet. Lights on water visible through gap in clouds.

It is interesting to remember that when an

Airship sets out for a long-distance voyage, carrying her maximum allowance of petrol, she can only rise to a limited height at the outset of her journey without throwing some of it overboard as ballast. As she proceeds on her voyage she can, if so desired, gradually increase her height as the petrol is consumed by the engines.

For this reason the next few hours will form one of the most anxious periods during our journey, as Scott, with 4900 gallons of petrol on board, weighing 15·8 tons, has to keep his ship as low as possible, and at the same time pass over a part of Scotland in the darkness where, at some points, the hills rise to a height of over 3000 feet.

2.8 *a.m.*—We are in thick cloud, and estimate our position to be over Inchkeith in the Firth of Forth, due north of Leith. Course 325°.

2.12 *a.m.*—Crossed coastline: just visible through gap in clouds. All is now more or less plain sailing, as we can make out the Firth of Forth. Passing over Forth Bridge and Rosyth, which shows up clearly—a blaze of lights. Train underneath plainly visible, not only from glowing funnel but also white smoke. Height 1500 feet.

2.13 *a.m.*—Rosyth is a beautiful sight—a fairyland of light. Ships in docks and ships moored in Firth plainly visible. Scott reduces height to 1200 feet.

2.15 *a.m.*—Heading up Firth of Forth.

2.20 *a.m.*—Visibility now quite good, and nature of country on both banks easily distinguishable.

2.25 *a.m.*—Wireless signal from General Groves, Deputy Chief of Staff, Air Ministry: " To General Maitland, Major Scott, Officers and Crew of R 34: All success to your flight and good luck to all on board.—R. M. GROVES."

Estimated speed over ground fifty-five knots, or sixty-six miles per hour.

Following wind of about twenty-five miles per hour.

2.27 *a.m.*—Wireless signal from H.M.S. *Furious*: " All good wishes from Captain and Flying Squadron."

Feeling very warm in our flying suits and silk underclothing, which have been specially supplied for this journey.

2.30 *a.m.*—Getting light—very streaky and dirty-looking sky. Following Firth of Forth and Clyde Canal just south of hills in Stirlingshire, where the highest hill is 1870 feet. Visibility good, clouds about 2500 feet. Stratus—wind about twenty-five miles per hour N.E. by N. Clouds as we go west seem to be becoming more compact, and taking more shape. Got away with 4900 gallons of petrol, which should give us an endurance of 4000 miles at an average air speed of thirty-seven knots, or 45 m.p.h.

2.45 *a.m.*—Passing under black ominous-looking rain-cloud 1000 feet above us. High hills on starboard beam causing bumps and making ship pitch slightly.

2.50 *a.m.*—Glasgow on port beam—a big blaze of light.

Following course of Clyde due west.

2.55 *a.m.*—Inchinnan on port beam about four miles away. (Inchinnan is of special interest to us, as it is R 34's birth-place, where she was built by Messrs. Beardmore, of Dalmuir.)

It is more or less light now, and high hills to the north show up very clearly. Weather behind us looking black as ink—we seem to be getting into better weather by going west.

3 *a.m.*—Magnificent view of Loch Lomond. Violent bumps off Dumbarton hills bring big strains on ship, particularly upon her elevators and rudders. Strong vertical currents of air. Ship alternately up by the bow and by the

OUTWARD JOURNEY 11

stern. All movements very slow and gradual. Nothing sufficient to cause seasickness (or should I call it "airsickness"?). Gorgeous scenery on starboard beam. Ship at one moment 24° up by the bow, and liquid in inclinometer has disappeared altogether! This is the biggest angle we have yet experienced, and it becomes necessary to hold on. Harris, our Meteorological Officer, says that an Airship travelling at 6000 feet would be quite above all these disturbances; but we cannot afford to go to that level at the commencement of a long voyage like this, as we don't want to lose any gas from expansion.[1] These "bumps" are, without doubt, caused by the high hills to the north, and are mainly katabatic in origin. Great masses of air piling up against the hills are forced upwards, become cooled, and descend on the other side, displacing the warmer air at the foot of the hills, thus causing squalls, "bumps," and generally unstable conditions. They will be met with nearly always in this region when the wind is from either S.W. or N.E.

3.8 *a.m.*—Over Greenock—following Clyde at 1500 feet—and picking our way through the

[1] See Appendix VI, p. 167.

hills. We carefully avoid going over 1500 feet, and so save losing gas. Average speed over ground during last hour sixty miles per hour, which is good considering the bumpiness of the air.

3.15 *a.m.*—Wonderful panorama of mountains over Loch Lomond, gradually getting salmon-pink as the sun begins to appear in the east—pink sky silhouetted near mouth of the Clyde, which, at this point, is about a mile wide.

Heading in southerly direction down Clyde with wind now astern and the Isle of Arran ahead—a very mountainous island. " Bumps " again troublesome.

3.20 *a.m.*—Passing over oil steamer going up the Clyde—the crew wave us a greeting.

3.30 *a.m.*—Sunrise over lowest point of Bute. Very big storm over mainland on port beam, and very dirty-looking weather ahead; we steer slightly to the west to avoid it. Wind estimated to be fifteen miles per hour from N.E.

Major Pritchard begins to get active with camera.

Discovered comfortable perch on top of fresh-water tank in forward car—glad to sit down.

3.45 *a.m.*—Passing over small island called

OUTWARD JOURNEY

Holy Island, 1000 feet high, with sheer precipice on both east and west sides.

Average speed making good fifty-eight knots. Altered course 260°.

The occupants of the forward car in this particular watch are—

Sgt. Watson .	. Steering.
S.M.2 Mayes	. Elevators.
Major Scott .	. In command.
Major Cooke	. Navigating Officer.
Capt. Greenland	. 1st Officer.
Major Pritchard	. Special Duties.
Lieut. Harris	. Meteorological Officer.

4 *a.m.*—Meteorological Officer climbs to roof of Airship 100 feet above us to gaze upon the sky, and returns, somewhat breathless from his exertions, with a generally favourable report.

4.20 *a.m.*—Off the most south-westerly point of Mull of Cantyre—ship steady—sea calm. Conditions and prospects extremely good.

4.35 *a.m.*—Had fifteen minutes' sleep in forward car sitting on fresh-water tank.

Off Rathlin Head, N.E. coast of Ireland.

Stopped forward engine—thirty-eight knots air speed on the remaining four.

4.45 *a.m.*—Passing over Rathlin Island. A

green little island with very fine precipitous cliffs—half-moon shape.

There is a lighthouse built at the west point of this island, and the whole cliff appears to have been strengthened with concrete.

In the distance we see a thick ground mist over N. coast of Ireland, indicating quiet weather conditions.

We send following message by wireless to Air Ministry at 4.52 *a.m.*—

" Off Rathlin Island, N.E. coast of Ireland, heading for Atlantic—all well.—Scott, R 34."

5 *a.m.*—Heading out towards Atlantic.

One last word with Meteorological Officer, who says weather conditions and prospects extremely good, and so to bed, with a comfortable feeling of confidence. Hammock berth No. 11 has been allotted to me : a nice deep, roomy hammock— but slung very high. Had to get passing member of the crew to give me a leg up—mentally resolved I must be more agile next time. Getting in is quite an acrobatic feat, and falling out is better avoided in a Service Airship like R 34, because there is only a thin outer cover of fabric on the underside of the keel on either side of the narrow walking way, and the luckless individual

OUTWARD JOURNEY

who tips out of his hammock would in all probability break through this fabric cover and soon find himself in the Atlantic.[1]

5.25 *a.m.*—Inisshtrahull Island one mile abeam to starboard. This is the last land we shall see.

6 *a.m.*—Airship running on four engines only, at 1600 revolutions.

Forward engine is being given a rest.

Air speed thirty-eight knots—making good 56·7 land miles per hour.

Course steered 298° N., 62° W.

Course made good 289° N., 71° W.

Wind N.E., 12 m.p.h. Height, 1500 feet.

Large banks of white fleecy cloud now come rolling in from the Atlantic, gradually blotting out all view of the sea. At first we are above these clouds, but gradually they rise higher, and we plough our way into the middle of them.

On leaving East Fortune a depression was centred over the southern part of the North Sea, with the result that it would be bound to extend as far as the W. coasts of Scotland and Ireland; and so cloud and rain must be expected till we get well away into the Atlantic.

7 *a.m.*—Plugging away steadily into the fog—

[1] See note, p. 34.

nothing visible or audible, not even the sea. Ship now becomes very heavy, due to rain and cooling down after superheating.[1] Scott keeps her 12° up by the bow in order to maintain a steady height.

This kind of weather in particular makes one realize the essential importance of navigation in all its forms, as we cannot see a yard ahead of us. Suddenly we catch a glimpse of the sea through a hole in the clouds, and notice we have a slight drift to the south, already estimated by both Scott and Cooke.

As rain becomes heavier Scott tries to get down below the clouds, but these prove to be too low, and it is discovered that these clouds are drier low down than up top.[2]

It is now breakfast time, and we sit down to this meal in two watches—fifteen in each watch.

In the officers' living-room the first watch for breakfast includes Scott, Cooke, Pritchard (Air Ministry Technical Observer), Lansdowne (United States Naval Airship Service), Shotter (Engineer Officer), and Harris (Meteorological Officer).

[1] See Appendix VI, p. 167.
[2] This was later found to be the general rule, the wettest part of a cloud being the top, and should be of great interest to pilots flying through rain when it is impossible or inadvisable to climb high enough to get above the clouds.

MAJOR SCOTT, AFTER SOLUTION OF THE PROBLEM.

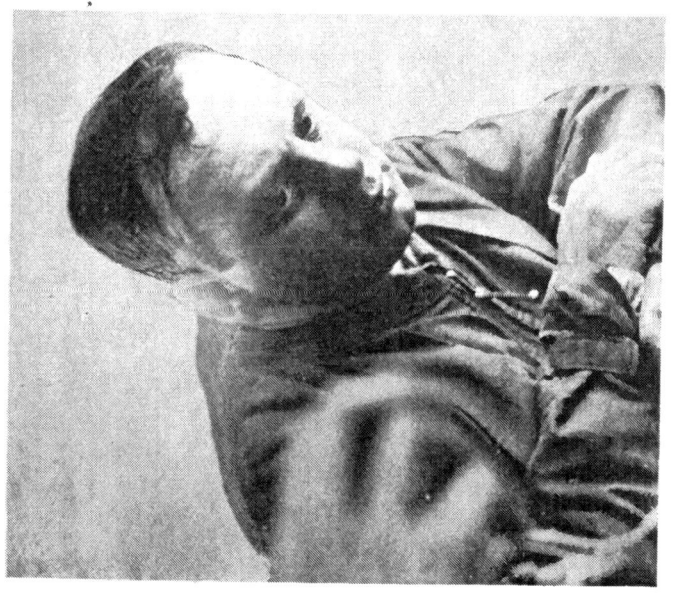

MAJOR SCOTT, BEFORE SOLUTION OF THE PROBLEM.

OUTWARD JOURNEY

We discuss R 34's recent flight up the Baltic, and are all unanimous that large Rigid Airships— even in high winds—are *much* steadier over the sea than surface ships; and agree that, in the future, people who are bad sailors will prefer to make the long sea passages by Airship if only to avoid seasickness.

In the adjoining compartment the gramophone is entertaining the crew to the latest Jazz tunes, such as "The Wild, Wild Women," etc. !

Still in thick fog, cold and damp. We compare our dangers with those of surface ships. Beyond its discomfort, this fog does not worry us in the least; besides, an Airship always has the alternative of climbing above it should she wish to do so, which need not be always the case. The surface ship has the iceberg to fear, but these have no terrors for us. No iceberg over 700 feet has ever been seen in N. Atlantic, 200 feet being considered a high one. High icebergs have been known in the Southern Hemisphere up to 1100 feet.

7.48 *a.m.*—Wireless message from H.M.S. *Tiger*[1]

[1] The two battle cruisers *Tiger* and *Renown* have been specially detailed to remain in the Atlantic during both the outward and homeward journeys, to assist us with weather reports.

via Ponta del Garda : " Lat. 56° 15′ N., Long. 36° 20′ W., Barometer 30.33, falling slowly; wind S.S.W., under 5 m.p.h. Thick fog bank. Visibility nil. Sea moderate."

8.10 *a.m.*—From Air Ministry : " What is your position ? "

Replied : " Position 55° 22′ N., 10° 40′ W. Course west; forty knots."

9 *a.m.*—Nothing but fog, estimated by Harris, the Meteorological Officer, to go down to within 150 feet of the water.

Five minutes later we find ourselves right out above the fog—height still 1500 feet—and beneath a cloudy sky with clouds at about 8000 feet. We are therefore in between two layers of clouds; a condition in which Alcock and Brown found themselves on more than one occasion during their recent Atlantic crossing from west to east. An excellent cloud horizon now presents itself on all sides, of which Cooke, our Navigating Officer, at once takes advantage. These observations, if the cloud horizon is quite flat, often prove a valuable rough guide, but cannot be regarded as accurate unless one can also obtain a check on the sun by day, or moon and stars by night. Cooke reckons it is easy to make as

OUTWARD JOURNEY

much as a fifty-mile error in locating one's position when using a cloud horizon as substitute for a sea horizon. Sky above clearing, and large patches of blue sky appearing. Temperature has risen to 60° Fahrenheit. Passing through this thick cloud the ship has collected a considerable quantity of electricity, with the result that the wireless operators report unpleasant electric shocks. Airship is probably negative and the cloud positive, causing slight discharge from the cloud to the ship. Scott and Greenland check standard compass on top of ship with compass in forward control car, and find they agree.

10 *a.m.*—Scott brings ship down to the 1300-foot level into the cloud bank, as she is beginning to heat up and gas-bags are full. This will have the effect of keeping her temperature down, and so avoid losing gas. Even clouds have their uses!

Cooke has three independent and specially constructed chronometer watches, which he carefully checks one against the other, and with which he will keep dead accurate Greenwich time with us throughout the voyage. This is essential to assist him in plotting his exact position.

10.38 *a.m.*—Still driving away into the fog at 1300 feet. Course N.W. by W., 298°. Speed through air forty knots; running on four engines at 1600 revolutions. Petrol consumption fifty-two gallons per hour. Course made good is slightly south of Great Circle owing to slight southerly drift, viz., 18° as measured on drift indicator.

Scott is able by skilful handling to keep the ship in these thick clouds to avoid superheating. At the same time, he judges it so nicely that Cooke, standing on the top of the ship, is able to get observations with sextant on sun and cloud horizon—his eye being practically on a level with the cloud horizon, the only thing peeping up above the top of the cloud-bank being the top of his head, which is functioning in the same way as a submarine periscope!

What a strange sight it would have been to another passing aircraft to see a man's head skimming along the top of a cloud-bank at forty knots!

10.45 *a.m.*—Restarted forward engine—1600 revolutions.

Stopped two aft engines. Speed thirty-two knots.

One method we use for calculating drift is to look down vertically through a bomb-sight,

OUTWARD JOURNEY

having previously set the instrument to the course the ship is steering. Then, by getting the top of a wave moving parallel to the lines in the bomb-sight, one can read off on the dial the actual course made good. Subtract from this the course steered, and one gets the angle of drift.

10.50 *a.m.*—Our wireless on 1400 metre wave is being jammed by local spark vessels.

10.56 *a.m.*—Stopped forward and two aft engines, and now running on only the two wing engines at 1600 revolutions. Air speed thirty knots, or 36 m.p.h., which is the most economical speed for this type of Airship, as she only consumes twenty-five gallons of petrol per hour on the two wing engines. Wind is east, seven miles per hour, and so we are making good forty miles per hour, with three engines resting.

Fog still thick, and visibility nil. Water dripping in through roof. Temperature 54° F. Cold and damp.

Cooke busy working out our exact position on chart by abstruse calculations and formulæ.

11 *a.m.*—Got a Directional Wireless Bearing on Clifden; but when we wanted another we could not get it, as they were not sending but receiving (presumably from Glace Bay). Unless

Clifden actually happens to be *sending* a message they are of practically no help whatever to aircraft trying to get a bearing on them with Directional Wireless, because when receiving they only acknowledge with single letters, and this does not give time to get an accurate sound direction.

Apparently the sole function of Glace Bay and Clifden is to transmit wireless messages of all kinds across the Atlantic; and so it would seem that in the future, when their number would justify the expense, W.T. Directional Stations will be required *solely* for the use of aircraft.

11.15 *a.m.*—Our position is now: Longitude 10° N., and Latitude 14° 40′ W., *i.e.* 400 miles from East Fortune, and 200 miles out into the Atlantic from Bloody Foreland. There is practically no wind, and we are making quite a good air speed with our two engines only. Pitôt tube gets filled up with fog and rain, and needs hauling in and blowing out occasionally, to get true readings.

W.T. arrangements are that we communicate with East Fortune as long as possible, and then— when they fade out—we shall still have Pem-

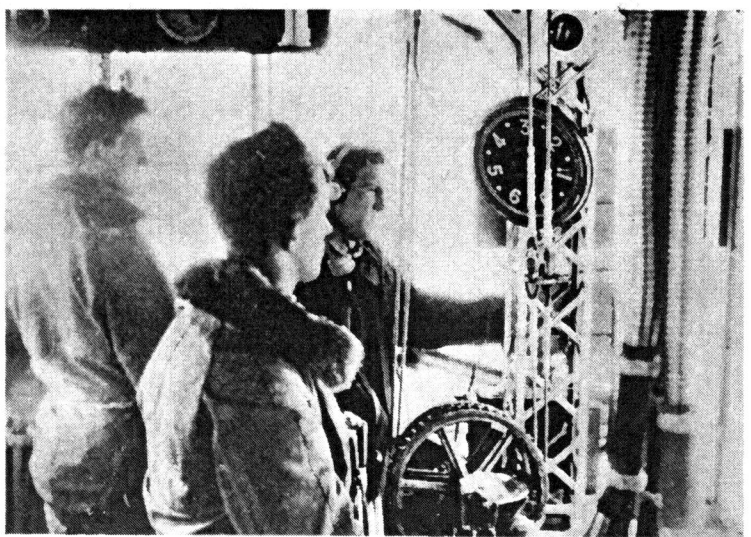

CONTROL CAR.

Flight-Sergt. Watson steering. Flight-Sergt. Mayes at the elevator wheel. Altimeter (large dial) needle shows that the ship is at about 1,200 feet above the sea.

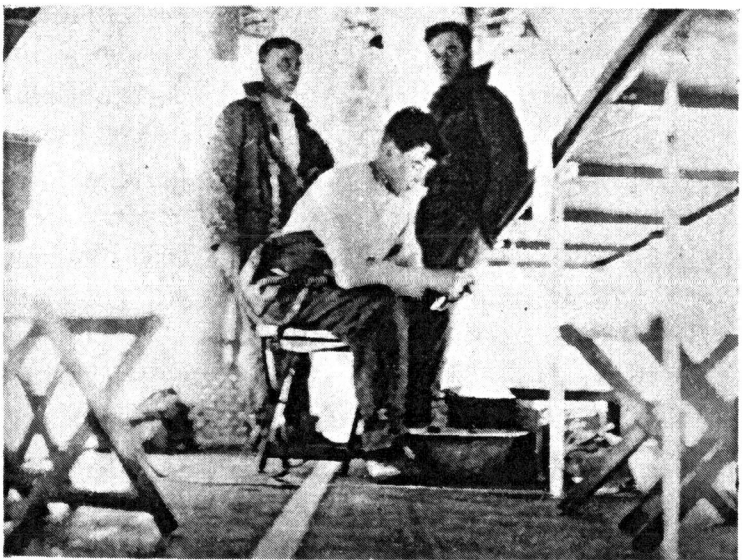

CREW SPACE INSIDE HULL.

One of the crew peeling potatoes for dinner. Lieut. Shotter and Sergt. Gent in background.

OUTWARD JOURNEY 23

broke, then Ponta del Garda (Azores), and finally Glace Bay.[1]

11.45 *a.m.*—Fog thicker and thicker, and we can see nothing, so think lunch would be a good idea. Excellent beef stew and potatoes. Caley's chocolate. Cold water to drink.

We compare our views on the distribution of air-pressure on the western side of the Atlantic, the winds we are likely to meet with, the fog we are likely to run into, the advantages of Directional Wireless for navigational purposes, cloud horizons, etc.

Scott, Cooke and Harris in comparing their experiences and expounding their theories are most interesting.

During meal-times ship is inclined to get an angle slightly down by the bow, owing to officers' and crew's dining quarters being situated too far forward. This must be corrected in future designs. Necessary to send some of the crew aft to correct trim. I notice they don't forget to take their food with them!

12 *noon.*—Watch off duty turn in for their routine four hours' sleep before coming on for their next turn of duty—only two hours in

[1] See map, Appendix VII.

this case, as it is the first of the two "dog" watches.

The sleeping arrangements consist of a hammock for each man off watch, suspended from the main girder of the triangular internal keel, which runs from end to end of the ship.

In the keel are situated the seventy petrol tanks, each of seventy gallons capacity, also living quarters for officers and men. In addition there are storage arrangements for lubricating oil, engine spares, water ballast, food, drinking water, etc. The latter form quite a considerable item, as will be seen from the following table of weights—

Petrol	. 4900 gallons =	35,300 lbs =	15·8 tons
Oil	. 230 gallons =	2,070 lbs =	·9 ,,
Water Ballast	. . . .	.	3 ,,
Crew, Luggage, Bedding, Food, etc.	. .	.	4 ,,
Spares	. . .	550 lbs =	·2 ,,
Drinking Water	. 80 gallons =	800 lbs =	·42 ,,
			24·32 tons

Decide to "turn in" and get some sleep.

It is quite hot in the keel, so sleep in underclothing only, outside sleeping bag—too hot inside. Slept soundly till 2.45 p.m., and feel much rested.

OUTWARD JOURNEY

2 *p.m.*—Cooke obtains observations for drift on surface of sea, the first since 5 a.m.

Scott comes to my hammock to tell me that there is a stowaway on board.

Just before starting it had been decided that one of the members of the crew (A.C.2 W. W. Ballantyne) must be left behind, the numbers being limited of necessity to thirty.

Ballantyne, on his own confession, hid himself in the darkness high up above the keel, on one of the longitudinal girders between the gas-bags, and has just emerged from his hiding-place.

He says he could not bear the thought of being left behind. Cannot help sympathizing with his motive, but it is bad from a disciplinary point of view, to say nothing of risking the success of the flight. Without his weight we could have carried 200 lbs. more petrol, and of course he has been allotted neither food nor hammock.

Had there been land beneath us instead of ocean we would put him off at once in a parachute; but as we are now well out in the Atlantic, there is nothing for it but to take him across, and make the best use of his services.

Necessary disciplinary action will be deferred until we arrive in America.

3.15 *p.m.*—Sea now visible at intervals through the clouds—a deep blue in colour, with a big swell on. Height 900 feet. Course 320°. Making good 299°. Our shadow on the water helps us to measure the drift angle, which both Scott and Cooke work out to be 21°. Running on forward and two aft engines only. Air speed thirty-six knots, or five knots more than we were getting with the two wing engines only.

Temp., 52° F.

Clouds rolling rapidly by, and patches of sky free of cloud gradually becoming larger indicate that we shall probably run into clearer weather.

3.30 *p.m.*—Durrant, our Wireless Officer, reports he has just spoken St. John's, Newfoundland, who, though very faint, proceed to send us a weather report. As we are still in touch with East Fortune and Clifden,[1] and have been exchanging signals with the Azores since reaching the Irish coast, our communications are, so far, admirable. Very beautiful rainbow effect on the clouds: one complete rainbow encircles the ship, and another smaller one encircles our shadow on the water; both are very vivid in their colouring. Colours in sequence from centre

[1] See map, Appendix VII.

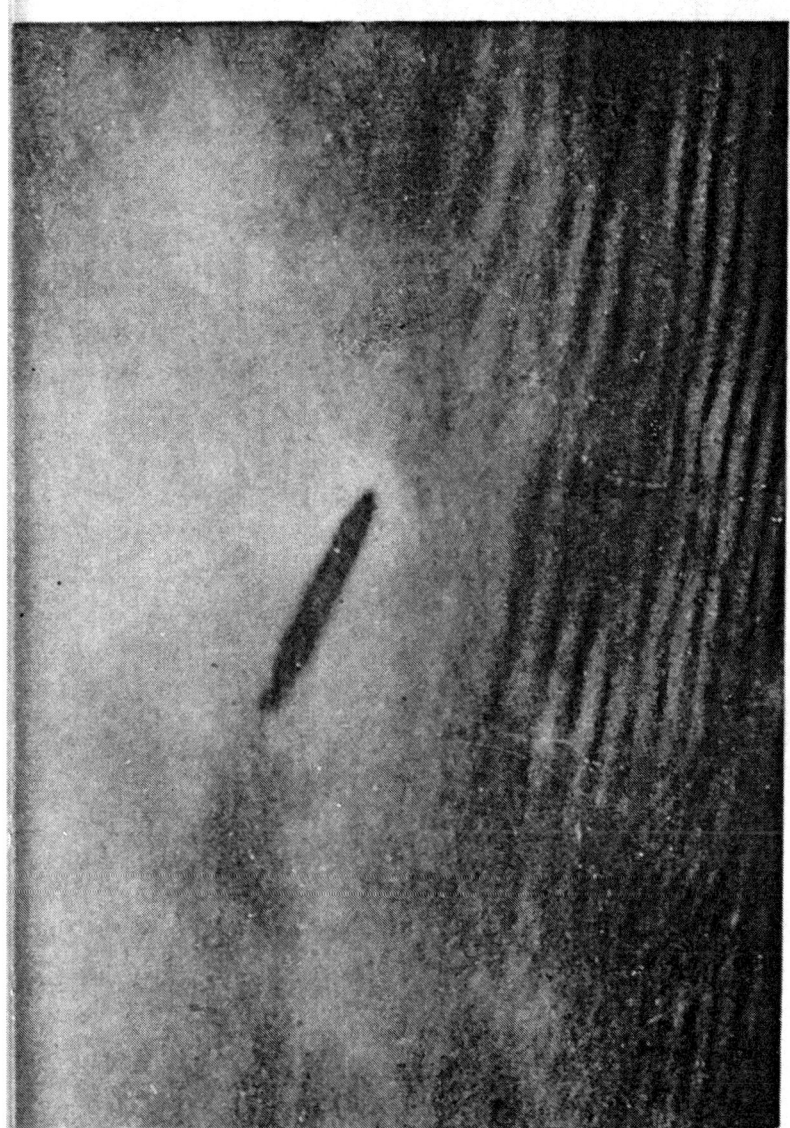

Shadow of R 34 thrown upon a Low Bank of Curiously Banded Clouds.

A complete rainbow is also shown round the bows, appearing like a halo.

OUTWARD JOURNEY

of circle: white, yellow, pink, dark blue, green, yellow, pink, green, yellow, pink, green. This rainbow or "glory" seems to be only evident when clouds are thin, and sea can be almost discerned through them.[1]

3.45 p.m. *Tea-time.*—Bread and butter, greengage jam and two cups of scalding hot tea, which has been boiled over the exhaust pipe "cooker" fitted to the forward engine. "Fruitarian" cake is also tried for the first time. It has rather a sickly taste, but is very sustaining; the whole assisted by Miss Lee White on the gramophone!

Greenland, the First Officer of the ship, is vainly trying to discover the culprit who used his toothbrush for stirring the mustard at lunch! Found a tabby kitten in forepart of keel, and recognized it as the one that was with us on our 21-hour flight from Inchinnan to East Fortune. There are also two carrier pigeons on board, and it is rather a question as to what use they can ever be, and what we had better do with

---

[1] We refer to the *Meteorological Glossary*, which tells us that this is a diffraction effect due to the bending of the rays of light round the minute water drops of which the clouds are composed.

them. Pigeons only fly overseas in the direction in which they have been trained, and, as these have been trained in the North Sea to fly west, they would presumably fly towards America directly we let them go, regardless of whether they could do the distance or not.

We decide to keep them on board and — if not necessary to use them on outward journey — to release them in sight of Ireland on return journey to see if they would (*a*) fly towards land if they could see it, (*b*) get on from Ireland to England. Anyway, if not released at all, they can claim to be the first pigeons to fly (?) the Atlantic!

4.45 *p.m.*—Cooke gets another observation of sun to cloud horizon.

Still in fog and low clouds. Sea not visible. Breaks in cloud not so frequent as previously. Height 1000 feet. Air speed thirty-five and a half knots on all five engines making good about thirty knots. Temp., 54° F.

4.50 *p.m.*—H.M.S. *Queen Elizabeth* picks us up on wireless and passes on following message to Air Ministry: " Position 53° 50′ N., 18° 00′ W.—all's well."

5 *p.m.*—Messages are received from both H.M.

R 34 Flying just above Dense Clouds on the Outskirts of a Depression.

This illustration shows a typical cloud horizon.

OUTWARD JOURNEY

battle cruisers *Tiger* and *Renown*, which have been sent out previously by the Admiralty into the Atlantic to assist us with weather reports and general observations.

They report respectively as follows—

H.M.S. *Tiger*: " Position 36° 50′ N., 36° 15′ W. Barometer, 1027 millibars—falling slowly—thick fog."

H.M.S. *Renown*: " Position 60° N., 25° W. Barometer, 1027 millibars—falling slowly—cloudy —visibility four miles."

Harris's deductions from these reports, coming, as they do, one from the S. Atlantic and the other from the neighbourhood of Iceland, are to the effect that there is no steep gradient, and that therefore there is no likelihood of any strong wind in those regions. Occasional glimpses of sea through fog. Have seen very little of the Atlantic on this flight so far. Tramp steamer s.s. *Ballygally Head*, outward bound from Belfast, destination Montreal, picks up our wireless on her Marconi spark set, which has a range of about thirty miles only. She gives her position as Long. 54° 30′ N., Lat. 18° 20′ W., and reports as follows : " Steering S. 80° W. true. Wind N. Barometer 30.10—overcast. Clouds low.—SUFFREN,

Master." They can hear us but cannot see us, and are very surprised to pick us up. We tell them we are R 34 bound for New York, and they wish us every possible luck. Her position when worked out was about thirty miles away, and at the extreme range of her wireless.

5.20 *p.m.*—Altered height to 1200 feet. Blue sky above. We can see nothing forward or downwards.

5.35 *p.m.*—Cooke trying to take observations on sun with bubble sextant, but is not successful—the sun being too high. Fine cloud horizon. Sea still invisible.

5.40 *p.m.*—Scott increases height to 2000 feet, to fill the gas-bags, which have cooled down. At this height we find ourselves well over the clouds, and the view is enchanting—as far as the eye can see a vast ocean of white fleecy clouds, ending in the most perfect of cloud horizons.

There is a cloudless and deep blue sky overhead, and now occasionally we get glimpses of vivid blue sea through gaps in the clouds beneath. Our Navigator does not miss this opportunity, and at once gets busy taking observations with sextant of sun and cloud horizon.

We feel in a world of our own up here amidst

Sunset—Still above the Clouds and nearing Centre of Depression

Above the worst of the Depression soon after Sunset

OUTWARD JOURNEY

this dazzling array of snow-white clouds. No words can express the wonder, the grandeur, or the loneliness of it all; one must experience these joys for oneself before one can even begin to realize them.

Two particularly fine specimens of "windy cirrus" cloud now appear on our port beam, and are clearly silhouetted at an enormous height against the azure sky.

These cirrus clouds (officially known as "Cirrus Ventosus") are very distinctive—little curly clouds like a black-cock's tail feathers.

Specimens of "Flocculent Cirro Stratus," rather resembling a diamond tiara, high in the centre and sloping away on both sides, also begin to appear away to the south. The appearance of these two types of cloud are interpreted by Harris as a first and infallible indication of a depression coming up from the south. We think that this depression may help us, provided we have crossed its path in advance.[1]

[1] In the Northern Hemisphere winds inside a depression blow anti-clock-wise. Consequently on the north side of a depression when flying the Atlantic there should be an easterly wind, a westerly wind being expected on the south side.

So far as we know, this generally accepted meteorological

It is interesting to note that, as yet, we have received no notice of any depression coming up out of the south in any weather reports.

Scott thinks we are making better headway up here above the clouds than we were when inside the clouds; though he cannot yet, of course, be certain of this.

5.50 *p.m.*—" Cirrus Ventosus " cloud has now gradually straightened out into a long thin curve known as " Band Cirrus." Height 1800 feet.

6.40 *p.m.*—Put back clock half an hour to corrected Greenwich mean time. Time is now 6.10 p.m., and we have covered 610 sea miles, measured in a direct line, in seventeen hours at an average speed of thirty-six knots, or 40 m.p.h. Position : Long. 53° 50′ N., Lat. 20° 0′ W.

Alcock and Brown finished their flight of 1800 miles in sixteen hours. We have now taken seventeen hours for 610 miles, so that their speed made good is three times as fast as ours. They, of course, were flying from west to east with a following wind behind them, while we are flying in the reverse direction with the prevailing wind

---

rule has never been turned to practical use by aircraft before, and we had the satisfaction of doing so both on the outward and homeward journeys.

FIRST GLIMPSE OF ATLANTIC AFTER PASSAGE OF CYCLONE.

NEXT MORNING. THE CALM AFTER THE STORM.

OUTWARD JOURNEY

against us. It will be noticed that our speed is distinctly low, but we have been running for a large part of the time on only three engines, with two engines resting. It must be remembered that Scott has to nurse his engines for the return journey, and had it not been for this, our speed for this outward journey could have been a third as fast again. At this rate, if all goes well, and if that depression from the south does not interfere, we should see St. John's, if not shrouded in fog (as it usually is) about midnight to-morrow, July 3rd.

7 *p.m.*—Wireless message from Air Ministry via Clifden: " Are you in touch with *Tiger* and *Renown*? Are you receiving from them weather reports, including upper air? "

We reply via *Renown:* " Yes, receiving from *Tiger*."

Message from Air Ministry continues : " Conditions unchanged in British Isles. Anti-cyclone persistent in Eastern Atlantic, a *new depression entering Atlantic from south*."

This confirms Harris's previous forecast at 5.40 p.m. on seeing the cirrus clouds, and is admirable proof of the accuracy and value of cloud forecasting.

We are all quite excited about this approaching depression, as it is exactly the weather conditions we were hoping to get. With any luck we should be benefited by the helping easterly wind on the north side of it, and, as we get further towards the Newfoundland coast, it should become more northerly, and blow us down towards New York.

Weather situation has therefore become extremely interesting, and it now remains to be seen whether our hopes and forecasts will be realized.

Our cooking arrangements are too primitive. Impossible to boil water slowly—can only boil fast. No frying facilities, which would be a boon—particularly for breakfast. No fresh vegetables on board. We must remember to get these, also fruit for the return journey, and generally arrange for more complete cooking arrangements on our next long-distance flight.[1]

The clouds have risen to our height, and we

---

[1] Future Airship liners will cater especially for the comfort of passengers; in fact, there is no reason whatever why the cuisine should not equal that provided on board any sea-going liner. Ample sleeping (and smoking!) accommodation will be available, and the passenger saloons heated throughout.

OUTWARD JOURNEY

are driving away through the middle of them, with no signs of the sky above or the sea beneath. Scott reckons the wind is N.E. by E., and helping us slightly.

7.30 *p.m.*—Cup of hot cocoa. Lay down for half an hour before evening meal, and read Emerson's Poems. Noticeable leakage from petrol tanks when ship takes up big angle by bow or stern, causing unpleasant smell of petrol vapour in keel. This must be remedied in future.

8 *p.m.*—Ship now very heavy—12° down by stern—owing to change of temperature. Running on all five engines, the idea being that it is more economical to burn petrol than to drop it as ballast. Height 3000 feet.

We are just on top of the clouds now—alternately in the sun, and then plunging through thick banks of cloud.

The sun is low down on the western horizon, and we are steering straight for it, making Pritchard at the elevators curse himself for having forgotten to bring tinted glasses.

Weather reports from E. Fortune, H.M.S. *Renown*, St. John's, Ponta del Garda (Azores), and Pembroke.

8.30 p.m.—Scott decides to descend below the clouds, and increases speed on all engines to do so. It is dark, cold, and wet in these clouds, and we shut all windows.

Cooke working out position from his last sun and cloud horizon observations: Height 2000 feet; sea not yet visible. Temp., 50° F.

8.45 p.m.—1500 feet. Sea now clearly visible through patches of fog, which Harris estimates will clear away altogether after sunset. Cooke gets drift observations on surface of sea, which give course and speed made good 265°, true forty knots. On this drift observation he was able to calculate the dead reckoning for the early morning star sights.

8.53 p.m.—We now find ourselves between two layers of cloud; one layer 1000 feet above us and another layer 500 feet below us, with occasional glimpses of the sea—very skilful handling and judgment on part of Scott.

8.55 p.m.—Sun is now setting, and gradually disappears below the lower cloud horizon, throwing a wonderful pink glow on the white clouds in every direction; a very beautiful sunset, and very cold.

9.10 p.m.—Turned in—feeling very tired and

OUTWARD JOURNEY

sleepy. Owing to early start have many hours of sleep to make up.

Thought out splendid scheme for getting into hammock: get good grip of main keel girder, pull up on the arms and then lower down into hammock from above—very quick and quite easy!

It is cold up here in the keel at night, but we feel very warm and snug in our sleeping bags.

All through this first night in the Atlantic the ordinary Airship routine, viz., navigating, steering, working the elevators, attending to the engines, etc., is continued, watch by watch, as in the daytime. The night is very dark, but the Airship is lit by electric light throughout, a much enlarged car lighting system having been fitted. There is a light to every instrument, which can be switched on as required, and, in case of failure of the lighting system, all figures and indicators are radiumized. This radium paint is so luminous that, in most cases, the lighting installation is unnecessary.

10.30 *p.m.*—Observation of Venus to cloud horizon.

10.45 *p.m.*—Weather reports come through from St. John's, Ponta del Garda, and Pembroke.

Up to date on whole journey Scott estimates we have used on an average 1·24 gallons of petrol per nautical mile made good. This, if it continues, should give us 1100 gallons of petrol, over and above, on our arrival in New York.

This, so far as we have gone, is an extremely good consumption figure, especially when one remembers how much we changed course to clear the high hills in Scotland.

Hope we shall be able to maintain this average; but have presentiment that we won't.

Thursday, July 3rd

2.56 *a.m.*—Last message from E. Fortune. We are now beyond their wireless range.

4.20 *a.m.*—Cooke obtains observations on the following stars: Polaris, Capella, Alpha and Romeda—all to cloud horizon. Height 2200 feet. Height above clouds 300 feet. This gives position as 52° 40′ N., 30° 15′ W., or about twenty-seven miles W.S.W. of dead reckoning position.

5.30 *a.m.*—We speak s.s. *Hellig Olav* bound for Copenhagen. She gives her position, 28° 10′ W.,

53° 10′ N. Wish we could see her instead of only talking to her.

9.20 *a.m.*—Clock put back another hour.

Position: Long. 35° 60′ W., Lat. 53° 00′ N., obtained by observations on sun and good cloud horizon—considered by Cooke to be accurate to within thirty to forty miles.

Making good thirty knots.

Wireless from Clifden: " Am requesting Glace Bay to pass all messages to you from us thirty minutes past odd hours."

We are now over the Westbound Steamship route from the Clyde to Cape Race, and momentarily crossing the Eastbound route from Belle Isle to Plymouth. We are well over half way between Ireland and Newfoundland, and are back again on the Great Circle route, having been slightly to the south of it, owing to the drift effect of a northerly wind.

If visible we should see Cape Race, Newfoundland, twenty-four hours from now—distance, 750 nautical miles.

Put this cheerful information up on notice board in dining-room.

Lieut. Shotter, Engineer Officer, who, through many causes, has been prevented from getting his fair share of sleep, is beginning to feel rather exhausted, and is dosed with aspirin by Luck, who is our amateur doctor for the voyage in addition to his duties as Third Officer.

Harris informs me that in his experience it either blows hard in the western Atlantic or there is fog. This may be regarded as an almost infallible rule.

9.17 *a.m.*—Got quite a nice view of Atlantic during short gap in clouds for about three minutes —sea a deep blue colour. Big swell. Visibility on surface of sea probably very good, but overcast. Estimated drift, 10 degrees. Height 900 feet. Running on forward and after engines only. Wind estimated to be S.E., about ten knots. Air speed thirty-three and a half knots.

Scott reckons we are making good thirty-eight knots and using roughly thirty-eight gallons of petrol an hour, which is quite a good state of affairs.

Scott's method of estimating wind on surface of sea is to watch a wave breaking, when foam is left on the surface, and the wave goes down wind. The foam then appears to move up wind, and the resultant effect gives you a more or less reliable direction of wind on surface of sea.

The *Aquitania* is, according to Marconi's Telegraph Communication Chart for July, now between Long. 30° and 20° W., or two-thirds of the way across to Ireland.

We should be hearing her soon, though we can only speak her on a relay, as our W.T. spark range is limited to 120 miles.

This same chart tells us that the following steamers should also soon be within range of our W.T. spark set: s.s. *Sardinian, Corsican, Saxonia, Minnekahda* and *La Savoie*.

We have passed within W.T. communication of s.s. *Mississippi, Mackinaw, Kirkholm, Canada, Michigan, Mesava, Mattwa, Orduna, Vestris, Manhattan, Rochambeau.* In addition, if in distress, we could probably get the s.s. *Sunderland* on our spark set, as she should be just within range.

We are in touch with Glace Bay for the first time.

9.35 *a.m.*—Wind seems to be increasing slightly, more white horses are beginning to appear, and, as our drift appears to be increasing too, this would be a further indication.

10 *a.m.*—Scott alters course a little to the north so as to be in position to use the easterly

wind on the north side of the approaching depression as much as possible.

10.15 *a.m.*—Weather report from St. John's: " Barometer 1010.2. Steady; temperature 44° F. Fog. Visibility about half a mile, fog seaward, wind westerly, very light." This is all right.

Turned in for an hour, but unable to sleep. Become absorbed in Kipling's story of " The Night Mail " in *Actions and Reactions*. Think I must have read this story fifty times! Every time I read it the more impressed I become with the reality of its prophecies, which give one that very same " atmosphere " of Aerial Liner travel that we are actually experiencing during every moment of this journey.

12 *noon.*—Midday meal—cold roast beef with one cold potato each. We are short of potatoes, having apparently eaten too many yesterday! Bread and butter, cheese, chocolate, and a cup of tea.

12.30 *p.m.*—Wind S.E. to S.E. by S. Strength fifteen to twenty knots. Clouds near surface of sea have cleared away, and we now have a visibility of about forty to fifty miles in all directions. Sky overcast with thin cloud.

This is really the first time we have had an all-

OUTWARD JOURNEY

round view of the Atlantic since we started. Sea is very blue, a biggish swell, and many white horses. Hope that, with this good visibility, we may at last see a passing ship.

One of the crew (a rigger) is ill. Temperature 102. Confined to hammock and dosed with quinine and salts.

Running on forward and after engines only, and resting both wing engines. Height 1100 feet. We cannot tell our height above sea accurately, as we don't know what the barometer is reading.

Our aneroid shows height as 1200 feet. Scott thought it more likely to be 1500 feet, as one cannot well assume that the barometer here on the surface of the water is the same as the barometer was when we left the ground at East Fortune.

We now try the experiment of lowering an instrument known as a sea-level aneroid, and specially designed to record atmospheric pressure readings, down to the surface of the water. The ship is not slowed down for the purpose in any way, and as this has not been tried before success is problematical.

Result is no good, as the instrument shows exactly the same reading on reaching car again as it had before starting. It had undoubtedly recorded the reading on surface, but got jerked (being a very sensitive instrument) on the quick haul-up.

Until we know our exact height above the sea we cannot plot our exact position, so until we speak a ship in our vicinity and get her barometer reading we still lack means for such a calculation. Some suitable method of getting this information must be perfected before we do any more long overseas flights.

Scott works out our height above the water in the following way—

The airship is throwing a very dark shadow on the surface of the sea on starboard side—almost immediately underneath the ship. By taking with a sextant the angle subtended by length of the shadow, and knowing the length of the shadow to be 640 feet, he gets the true height. In this case the height works out at 2100 feet, whilst the aneroid gives us only 1200 feet—a variation of 900 feet.

12.45 *p.m.*—Durrant is speaking s.s. *Canada* on our W.T. spark set. Another W.T. operator (Corporal Powell) is trying to get her on the directional wireless, so that we may know in

OUTWARD JOURNEY

what direction to look for her. All we know at the moment is that she is *somewhere* within 120 miles of us, and bound for Liverpool.

She gives her position as follows: " Long. 51° 16' N., Lat. 39° 42' W. (or sixty miles S.S.E. from us), barometer 30.8, rising. Wind and sea moderate from S.E.—DAVIS, Master."

Her wireless operator tells us that great enthusiasm prevails on board, and that every one is hoping to catch sight of us. This feeling is mutual, but, although we do our best to get her on our directional wireless, besides gazing through our glasses in every direction, she remains just beyond our visibility.

Scott now brings his ship down to the 1200-foot level, to try and find a more easterly trend in the wind.

The reading on s.s. *Canada's* barometer is of the greatest value, and is exactly the information of which we are in need. We can now work out our true height above the sea, and consequently fix our exact position. Her barometer on surface reads 30.8, whilst ours in the ship is 29.7. This shows a difference of 30.8–29.7, or 1.1 inches. Remembering the rule that for every 1000 feet you rise the barometer falls one inch, we get our height as 1000 feet, which tallies almost exactly with Scott's estimate of 900 feet inaccuracy mentioned above. It is quite possible that Scott's calculation of 900 feet may still be dead accurate, as s.s. *Canada* is some fifty or sixty miles away, and the change in barometer over that distance may well work out at 100 feet.

What a relief it is to remember that peace prevails and we need no longer keep sharp and constant look-out for enemy submarines!

Not being allowed to smoke is a great privation upon long flights of this description, and is acutely felt by all members of the crew, particularly after meals. Special arrangements to allow for this will be made on future long-distance Airship journeys.[1]

Harris unwisely shuts his hand in door of W.T. cabin—painful, but not serious. Flow of language not audible to me, as fortunately forward engine happened to be running!

1.30 *p.m.*—Conditions now very pleasant. Blue sky above and blue sea below—nice and warm. We remove nearly all our clothes and feel delightfully comfortable. Thank goodness there are no appearances to keep up on board our Aerial

[1] See note, p. 34.

OUTWARD JOURNEY

Liner; and we don't mind what we look like or who sees us!

Fine cirrus clouds on starboard beam.

Very big drift, estimated at 30°. Ship practically travelling sideways. Wind is estimated to be S.S.E., thirty knots, and helping us considerably. Scott calculates, by measuring angles on shadow with sextant, that we are making good forty knots. Cooke calculates with drift indicator that we are making good thirty-eight knots. I log accordingly our speed made good as thirty-nine knots, and so every one is satisfied!

Durrant hears *Aquitania*, but does not speak her.

St. John's reports wind easterly, which is good hearing.

1.50 *p.m.*—Trouble with starboard amidships engine. Engine stopped. No details as yet.

2.2 *p.m.*—Engine re-started. A small screw on water jacket had worked loose, and this has been made secure with a piece of copper sheeting and the entire supply of crew's chewing gum (which was hastily chewed first by Engineer Officer and two engineers!) We will never be without a good supply of this in future, and this should be a very good and unexpected advertisement for Mr. Edmondson's brand of chewing gum!

Scott and Cooke spend much time at chart table with protractors, dividers, stop-watches and many navigational text-books, measuring angles of drift and calculating course made good.

Whenever the surface of the sea is visible observations are taken with Drift Indicator to check our course and speed. This is also frequently checked by timing the ship's shadow when visible in passing some defined spot, such as foam left by a breaking wave.

Aerial navigation is more complicated than navigation on the surface of the sea, owing to the existence of a third dimension; but there is no reason why, when Directional Wireless has been perfected, and when we know more about the air and its peculiarities, it should not become very accurate.

2.10 *p.m.*—Wind rising—sea beginning to get rough—visibility one mile.

4 *p.m.*—We should soon be over the Canadian summer route of steamers bound for the St. Lawrence via Belle Isle Strait, and may perhaps sight a ship.

From our experience so far on this voyage, it

seems an absolute miracle to me that Hawker should have found a ship when he did in this vast Atlantic.

4.30 *p.m.*—We are now in the vicinity of the well-known Labrador current, and there are already indications of these cold currents in the fog which is beginning to appear above the surface of the water.

Cooke gets good observation of sun to sea horizon.

Wind which is now forty-five knots is "backing," and we are being carried rather far north and off the direct course we originally intended. Position now about due south of Greenland. Angle of drift about 50°.

Petrol expended, 1546 gallons. Petrol left, 3354 gallons.

6 *p.m.*—Observations of sun and moon to sea horizon give position as 58 miles N., 30° E. of D.R. position at 2.15 *p.m.* We are gradually getting further and further into the shallow depression which was reported yesterday coming up from the South Atlantic. For the last four hours the sea has been rising, and now the wind is S.S.E., about forty-five knots, and we are travelling sideways over the sea, making good

twenty-five to thirty knots. Harris thinks, when we have passed the centre of this depression, we should get a more easterly wind and clearer sky, so we go right ahead into it, and are full of confidence.

7 *p.m.*—All visibility now gone, and thick fog everywhere. It is unpleasantly cold; we are not only fully dressed, but wearing our overcoats as well. Conditions at present not at all nice, and it is an anxious time from now on, until we see how the weather develops.

We are a little over 300 miles from the nearest point of Newfoundland, viz., Trinity Bay, and 350 miles from St. John's. Estimated drift 70°. In all probability we should get across the centre of this depression in two or three hours' time.

It is raining very fast, which is a good sign, as it nearly always rains near the centre of a depression.

In spite of our drift angle of 70° we are making good a forward course direct on Belle Isle, which is at the most northerly point of Newfoundland, and the entrance to the Gulf of St. Lawrence.

White horses just visible occasionally through the fog. Sea very rough.

H.M.S. *Tiger* reports: " Wind S.E. by S.,

OUTWARD JOURNEY

twenty miles per hour, freshening. Squally sky. 2/10 Cirrus Stratus. 3/10 Stratus, misty to the S.W. Visibility ten miles. Sea moderate. Position Lat. 53° 50' N. Long. 40° W. Barometer 30.25, falling slowly."

7.10 *p.m.* Struck by fierce squall. Heavy rain. Ship remarkably steady considering intensity of squall. Scott remarked that he would not like to take a 23-class rigid into this.

The rain is driving through the roof of the fore car in many places, and there is a thin film of water over the chart table. The wind is roaring to such an extent that we have to shout to make ourselves heard.

7.30 *p.m.*—Time for evening meal, but no one gives it a thought while this entertainment is going on.

Scott gets his bald patch thoroughly soaked whenever he peeps out through window to try and watch direction of wind!

Am much struck by the steadiness of the ship in this squall, which is a very severe one. Beyond a gradual and very slow pitching, causing us to hold on and making everything slip about pretty considerably, we feel no inconvenience, and not the slightest symptoms of seasickness. The sea, on the other hand, when last we saw it, was very rough and I, for one, being the worst possible sailor, would certainly be feeling horribly ill if I were on board a surface ship!

Scott has consultation with Luck, his Third Officer, and decides to try and climb right out of this depression. Nose of ship put up accordingly.

8 *p.m.*—Our evening meal of bread and butter, cheese, and Oxo is a simple one, and not particularly appetizing. Resolve to take a personal interest in the food question for the return journey. We sit seven of us in a circle, Luck, Scott, Cooke, Lansdowne, Harris, Shotter and myself, talking about everything except Airships and storms in the Atlantic. For want of chairs Shotter and Lansdowne sit on the floor underneath the table—as good a place as any. The cat purrs contentedly in Harris' lap, with one eye always on the food!

8.30 *p.m.*—Just emerging over top of depression.

8.40 *p.m.*—Our height is now 3400 feet, and we are well out of the clouds and right out of the depression, exactly as foretold by Harris. The rain has ceased, and we are travelling quite smoothly again. This is probably the first time

OUTWARD JOURNEY

that the top of the danger area of a shallow depression has been scientifically observed and photographed from above. The lesson we learn from this is that the rain and wind usually to be expected within a "shallow" depression only prevail up to a low level, so that upon encountering such a depression, the best course is to seek a higher level and continue flying comfortably above it.

With a "deep" depression, upon the other hand, the higher you go the worse the wind and rain will undoubtedly become; and the best policy to pursue is to circumvent them and so turn them to useful advantage.[1]

To the west the clouds have lifted, and we see a most wonderful and interesting sky. Black, angry clouds above us, giving place to clouds of a grey mouse colour, then a clear and bright salmon-pink expanse, changing lower down the horizon to darker clouds with a rich golden lining as the sun sinks below the surface. The sea is not visible, and is covered by a fluffy grey feather-bed of cloud, slightly undulating, and extending as far as the eye can reach.

The moon is just breaking through the black clouds immediately above us. To the east we

[1] See note, p. 31.

see below us the black ominous depression from which we have just emerged, while away more to the south the cloud-bed over which we are passing seems to end suddenly and merge into the horizon.

The lessons to be learnt from this magnificent cloudscape are difficult at present to estimate. The sunset is a very stormy one, but this is not to be wondered at when actually inside a depression.

The sky ahead looks lighter, but the cloud-bed beneath us should be " packing " more, and not so " fleecy " if we are to get better weather. Perhaps it will " pack " more later on? We are collecting some valuable meteorological data on this flight without a doubt, and each fresh phenomenon as it appears is instantly explained by the ever-alert Harris, who astonishes us all with his meteorological knowledge under so many and varied conditions.

He possesses plenty of " imagination," and this seems to me to be an essential qualification for the art of reading the clouds and thoroughly appreciating their meaning.

9 *p.m.*—Clouds are all the time getting lower; fifteen minutes ago they were 3200 feet above the

water, now they are 2000 feet only, and it is possible that in half an hour's time they may have cleared away altogether, and allow us a clear view of the sea.

10 *p.m.*—One of the engineers—Sergt. W. A. Scull—is reported sick. Top portion of thumbnail torn and thumb badly bruised, caught in moving part of machinery. Very painful, but not serious. Says he will be all right to-morrow.

It is a remarkable fact that nearly every member of the crew owns a mascot of some sort or another. Shotter, the Engineer Officer, wears a pair of his wife's silk stockings as a muffler, and Scott's mascot is a small gold charm called " Thumbs up ! "

We speak s.s. *Megantic*. Message from Azores to say weather there is fine, which means that this depression evidently missed them, and is passing away in a N.E. direction up the Atlantic. This is the usual path of these depressions.

Friday, July 4th

1.29 *a.m.*—Message from St. John's : " Handley Page aeroplane probably leaving for New York at 10.30 a.m. to-day."

1.30 *a.m.*—We ask s.s. *Megantic:* " Is there D.F. Station at Cape Race ? "

Reply comes : " Yes, D.F. at Cape Race—Call V.C.E."

1.37 *a.m.*—From s.s. *Megantic:* "To Cape Race—Airship R 34 is calling you. Can you hear him ? "

1.40 *a.m.*—From Cape Race to all ships : " Urgent, stop transmitting—Government message."

Cannot help feeling how much more pleased we would be with our own importance if it wasn't so *very* temporary !

4.30 *a.m.*—Wonderful sunrise, the different colours being the softest imaginable, just like a wash drawing.

5 *a.m.*—Bad " atmospherics," telephones burn out—new pair rigged.

During the night no trouble has been experienced due to cooling down, as petrol consumed has counterbalanced loss of false lift.[1]

5.30 *a.m.*—Sun's altitude to cloud horizon gives position 50° 05′ N., 49° 27′ W. These are the first " sights " Cooke has been able to get since 6 p.m. yesterday.

7 *a.m.*—Sun no longer visible, and therefore

---

[1] See Appendix **VI**, p. 167.

only drift observations for checking position are possible.

Height 1000 feet. Bright blue sky above, thin fog partly obscuring the sea beneath us. Sea moderate. Big swell. The fog bank seems to end abruptly ten miles or so away towards the south, where the sea appears to be clear of fog, and a very deep blue. Standing out conspicuously in this blue patch of sea we see an enormous white iceberg. The sun is shining brightly on its steep sides, and we estimate it as roughly 300 yards square and about 150 feet high. As these icebergs sometimes cover an under-water area of between seven and nine times their height above the surface, we wonder whether it is aground, as depth of water at that point is only about 150 fathoms. Looking down upon this huge iceberg from the open window of the forward car we can clearly see treacherous green ice protruding under the water in all directions. As this under-water ice could, under no circumstances, be seen from a surface ship, it brings home to one the hidden dangers that ocean-going vessels are liable to meet with in this portion of the Atlantic, where fogs may be expected at all times of the year.

The Airship Liner of the future will undoubtedly have risks of collision with her sister liners of the air in the same way that ocean-going vessels have with one another, but—thank goodness!—we shall always be entirely immune from any iceberg risks, or from such enemies as rocks, reefs, or shoals.

As a matter of fact, our chances of collision in the air should be considerably less than those of sea-going vessels, because we will have another dimension to fall back upon and, in all probability, will fly at pre-arranged levels.

Another big iceberg can just be seen in the dim distance.

These are the only objects of any kind, sort, or description we have yet observed on this journey.

7.15 *a.m.*—Altered course for St. John's.

8.15 *a.m.*—Fog still clinging to the surface of the water, which therefore must be very cold.

Extraordinary crimpy wave-like appearance of clouds rolling down underneath us from the north. Harris has never seen this before. Pritchard gets photograph.

8.30 *a.m.*—Small iceberg a point or two off our

OUTWARD JOURNEY

starboard beam about fifty feet high and very close to us. Another photograph.

Other icebergs visible in the distance away to the south.

On our port beam there is a long stretch of clear blue sea sandwiched in between wide expanses of fog on either side, looking just like a blue river flowing between two wide snow-covered banks. Cause—a warm current of water which prevents cloud from hanging over it. This well illustrates the rule that over cold currents of water the clouds will cling to the surface.

From a purely flying point of view we would prefer clouds to be higher, so that we could get inside them and prevent superheating.[1] The clouds are, however, rising. We have watched them gradually increasing in size, from little wisps of vapour just above the water. They now assume definite shape, and we can be quite certain that they are rising. There is blue sky and a hot sun above, so Scott decides to try a lower level and get inside the clouds, where we are bound to cool down considerably.[2]

8.40 *a.m.*—We are now in touch with Cape

[1] See Appendix VI, p. 167.
[2] For disadvantages caused by superheating, see Appendix VI, p. 167.

Race, 250 miles away, on our spark transmitter set; they give us two directional bearings. We should soon be in touch with Canso, Nova Scotia.

Having burnt a lot of petrol the ship is light, so Scott has to force her down on the elevators to get her into the cloud-bank.

8.45 *a.m.*—W.T. message from Cape Race: "Your bearing at 8.15 a.m. 36 degrees east of true north."

We are now over a large ice-field—masses of broken ice floating on the surface in every direction. Take a turn with Pritchard at pumping petrol, which is a laborious and most unpleasant proceeding, and must be avoided in future ships. Feel slight symptoms of toothache.

9 *a.m.*—Ship down by the nose 15° to get down into the clouds, which are now just beneath us. Height 1500 feet. Clouds look rather "switchbacky" ahead, indicating presence of more icebergs.

Weather report from St. John's: "Wind N. three miles per hour. Drizzling. Visibility one mile."

Our position at 9 a.m.: Long. 49° 05' N., Lat. 30° 25' W. Sent to Air Ministry.

OUTWARD JOURNEY

9.5 *a.m.*—Enormous pieces of floating ice under us now; small icebergs in themselves. The ice is blue-green under water, with frozen snow on top, and the whole sea seems to be full of little blobs of cream in every direction—very pretty sight.

The fog is thickening as we get nearer the coast of Newfoundland, and only occasionally do we get a glimpse of the sea. We are now well inside the cloud-bank.

9.15 *a.m.*—A message reaches us from the Governor of Newfoundland : " To General Maitland, officers and crew, R 34 : On behalf of Newfoundland I greet you as you pass us on your enterprising journey.—HARRIS, Governor."

9.55 *a.m.*—Hardly have we replied when Cape Race say : " I have radios for you."

We answer : " Go ahead."

First message reads as follows : " To R 34, from Canadian Pacific Railway : Hearty greetings to the crew of R 34 on its initial trip across the Atlantic.—Can you give us any story, please ? —MACMILLAN, Manager of Telegraphs."

Similar messages come through,[1] and it strikes one as being rather strange that messages of

[1] See Wireless Log, Appendix V, p. 143.

congratulation should be coming in and duly pinned up on the notice-board in the dining-room from the countries we are struggling to reach, and long before we have even caught a glimpse of them.

11.50 *a.m.*—Still over drifting ice-field, making good headway. Scott much relieved at discovering this, as we haven't seen the sea for some hours and, for all any of us knew, we might have been making no headway at all. Our calculations now show that if we meet a stiff headwind going down the coast we may find ourselves in difficulties over petrol.

We must have been consuming more than we thought.

Latest check gives us 2222 gallons.

12.15 *p.m.*—Gas temperature is now 106 degrees, and air temperature 40 degrees—a difference of 66 degrees. This is the biggest differentiation between gas and air temperatures that we have ever yet experienced in the Airship Service. The reason the air is so cold is because we are over the Labrador current, and the sea is full of ice. The effect on the ship caused by this big differentiation in temperatures is to produce excessive superheating, and it becomes necessary therefore to increase height to 4000 feet in order to reduce this effect.

12.50 *p.m.*—Land in sight. Hooray!

First spotted by Scott on starboard bow: a few small rocky islands visible for a second or two through the clouds, and instantly swallowed up again.

Altered course S.W. to try and get a closer look at them.

Eventually make them out to be the north coast-line of Newfoundland. This is quite the most thrilling moment of our voyage—great excitement on board.

Whether or not we now succeed in getting through to New York, we have at any rate successfully accomplished the first stage of our adventure, and are the first to bridge the gulf from East to West by way of the air.

Those of us on duty in the forward car compare our method of crossing with that of Columbus over 400 years ago. How easy our task compared to what his must have been!

1 *p.m.*—Lunch—a cheery meal, and every one in the best of spirits.

1.30 *p.m.*—Crossing the coast-line—occasional glimpses of rocky cliffs and small islands through the fog. Message comes through via Cape Race: "To R 34 from Senior Naval Officer, St. John's: Request to be informed if you intend passing over St. John's, and if so what time?"

Reply: "Yes—probably about 4 p.m. G.M.T."

2.30 *p.m.*—We are passing over Newfoundland at 1500 feet, and the fog has momentarily cleared. Away to the east the country is flat: a mass of large and small lakes. The ground appears to be very rocky, with many large forests. The lakes look extraordinarily deep, and there appears to be water everywhere—goodness knows what the annual rainfall must be! The trees are thick, and one is struck by the number of dead trees both standing and lying on the ground.

To the west there are ranges of hills and big lakes, and we are travelling parallel with, and about thirty miles inland from the coast-line.

No signs of habitation or civilization anywhere; I've never seen such a bleak, barren country in all my life. After much calculation Cooke makes out we have crossed the coast of Newfoundland on the north-west side of Trinity Bay.[1]

---

[1] Kipling in his story "With the Night Mail" (*Actions and Reactions*), written as long ago as 1909, chose Trinity Bay as the point where his westward-bound aerial liner of

Desolate Country in the Interior of Newfoundland.

R 34 over the Town of Fortune when Letters were dropped by Parachute for the Governor of Newfoundland.

Dropped messages to Governor of Newfoundland and to Sir Robert Borden (Prime Minister of Canada) by parachute, on chance of their being picked up and delivered. Parachute and messages fall into huge forest, so it is a very forlorn hope.

Message from St. John's as follows: " Local authorities informed of your position and intention of passing over St. John's. Can we be of any assistance? Congratulations on successful voyage. Martynside aeroplane will attempt to join you."

To St. John's from R 34: " Tell Mr. Raynham to beware of long aerials hanging from R 34 when he gets near us."

3 p.m.—We are in thick fog again, with occasional glimpses of the country underneath.

Message from H.M.S. *Sentinel* giving us her position at easterly end of Bonavista Bay, and also giving us our position.

---

the future first strikes land, and now we, in the first aircraft to cross the Atlantic from E. to W., ten years later, first sight land at this same Trinity Bay. Mr. Kipling, to celebrate this coincidence, gave the writer a signed copy of his book and, in return, received the actual volume we carried on board, inscribed with the signatures of all the crew.

K

We are making good thirty-eight to forty knots, there being no wind on ground. Course set for Fortune Harbour.

In working out our time since leaving the Irish coast at Rathlin Island on July 2nd and crossing the coast of Newfoundland on July 4th, we discover we have flown the Atlantic land to land in exactly fifty-nine hours.

3.30 *p.m.*—Passing out of Fortune Harbour. Very picturesque—high cliffs with miles upon miles of forest coming right down to water's edge. Somebody remarks that most of these trees belong to Lord Northcliffe, and go to help produce *The Times* and *Daily Mail*. Very blue water, deep and transparent. Wonderful natural harbours and fiords—very like Norway. Little groups of hutments at each harbour with piles of cut timber, which appears to be the principal industry in the country, bar fishing.

Inhabitants gaze up at us (presumably in astonishment). They make no demonstration whatsoever. Nice little fishing village on promontory, a delightful collection of what look like tiny pink, blue and white dolls' houses!

Miles away, out to sea, looking right across the peninsula to the east, we can see a huge iceberg,

OUTWARD JOURNEY

with the sun gleaming on its perpendicular walls of ice.

Unpleasant neuralgic toothache at intervals—presumably a sign of fatigue.

3.45 *p.m.*—Message from Lt.-Col. Lucas [1] asking when we would land New York. Replied: " Early Sunday morning." We have still 870 miles to go.

3.55 *p.m.*—Little sailing ships under full sail look like toys on the Serpentine. Sea in this gigantic harbour deep blue. Flat calm—not a breath of wind. We see a Telegraph Office marked on our chart as the little town of Fortune, so decide again to drop messages to Governor of Newfoundland and others at that spot.

4 *p.m.*—Threw out messages, but parachute burst on opening.[2]

4.15 *p.m.*—The clock has been put back again. The sun is shining brightly, and the water on the S. of Newfoundland is a still deeper blue. Along the coast-line the water is completely transparent and a bright green right up to the beach: a gorgeous colour—green as any emerald. The

---

[1] See footnote, p. 83.
[2] We heard subsequently that these letters had been seen to fall in a meadow, and were picked up duly posted and received.

shades of green gradually darken as the water gets deeper, until they finally become the deepest of deep blue.

4.35 *p.m.* We are now over the two French islands Miquelon and St. Pierre, and are steering a course for Halifax, Nova Scotia.

We refer to the *Newfoundland and Labrador Pilot Book*, and read with particular interest the description of the Newfoundland cod fisheries, which are probably the finest in the world. This is also the happy hunting-ground for halibut and Mother Carey's chickens.

Air speed thirty-five and a half knots on forward and two wing engines. Fresh following wind of about ten miles per hour, so we are making good forty-five and a half knots on three engines, which is excellent.

The French flag flying over the signal station at St. Pierre is smartly dipped in salute as we pass over. Being taken completely by surprise we are unable to dip our " White Ensign " in response.

The reason is this : we fly our ensign right aft, and it takes quite an appreciable time to send a man to the after end of the ship to make a signal.

Smart fellow that French signaller—he certainly caught us out badly !

Shotter is a bit anxious over his petrol consumption figures, and is adding them up continuously.

7.30 *p.m.*—Message from General Seeley, Under-Secretary of State for Air : " Warmest congratulations to General Maitland and to all your gallant comrades. Best wishes for completion of voyage."

7.45 *p.m.*—We are now out to sea again, passing Nova Scotia, and over tramp steamer s.s. *Seal*, bound for Sydney. She is the first ship we have actually set eyes on throughout the whole of this journey.

Message from *Seal :* " Good luck. God speed."

8.5 *p.m.*—Clear weather. Making good twenty-seven knots on three engines, resting remaining two. Sea moderate. Wind now not so favourable.

8.15 *p.m.*—Land again in sight. Northerly point of Cape Breton Island, Nova Scotia. Lighthouse giving four flashes. We have averaged thirty-two and a half knots between Newfoundland and Nova Scotia. At this rate we should make Halifax 2.30 a.m. to-morrow.

8.30 *p.m.*—s.s. *Metagama* speaks us : " Hearty congratulations. Your progress watched with much interest—all success.—MILLER."

11 *p.m.*—We intercept Cape Race talking to the Handley-Page aeroplane,[1] piloted by Major Brackley and Rear-Admiral Mark Kerr, which is now starting to fly from St. John's to New York, where we all hope to foregather.

The messages are as follows—

From Cape Race: "How are you going on? Send V's for bearing."

From Handley-Page: "Going strong—85 m.p.h."

11.58 *p.m.*—Handley-Page signals break off suddenly.

12 *midnight.*—Intercepted on wireless that Dempsey had knocked out Jess Willard in third round for heavy-weight championship of the world! And so to bed.

Saturday, July 5th

2.30 *a.m.*—Very dark. The lights of white-haven show up brightly on our starboard beam,

---

[1] This machine and also the Martynside, piloted by Mr. Raynham, had been erected near St. John's, Newfoundland, and were awaiting a suitable opportunity to fly the Atlantic from west to east.

We discovered later that this was the approximate time of their crash in the darkness in Nova Scotia, caused by a petrol pipe breaking in one of their engines.

and we make out the lights of a steamer passing us to the east.

Two aft engines resting. Air speed thirty-six knots. Making good nothing. Strong head wind against us, and low cloud. Height 1000 feet. Returned to hammock! Too depressing! We are up against a wind barrage, which is probably peculiar to the east coast of Nova Scotia. It is typical of its kind, and Harris thinks it would be met with usually along this coast when wind is from a westerly quarter.

If only we had sufficient petrol we would now change course to the westward, crossing the American coast, and so get round behind this barrage.

Atmospherics very severe on W.T., but Powell and Edwards succeed in keeping watch notwithstanding.

3.45 *a.m.*—From Barrington Passage: " I have 700 words weather for you. Can I carry on or send it at intervals ? "

Reply from R 34: " Go right ahead."

5.58 *a.m.*—From Canso: " Your bearing 81° E. of us. Handley-Page aeroplane has crashed." We ask anxiously if any one is hurt, and are much relieved at getting a reassuring reply.

6 *a.m.*—Came down to 600-foot level to dodge wind.

7.10 *a.m.*—Crossed coast of Nova Scotia at Goose Island with a view to crossing the mainland into the Bay of Fundy, where we hope to find less wind. Miles and miles of endless forest. Here and there a clearing with a hut or two, some cattle, and an acre or so of cultivated ground. Any number of small rivers and lakes—inhabitants always seem to settle near the rivers. Marguerite daisies very pretty on all cleared ground.

Put the wind up a big brown eagle. The few people we see look up at us, but make no sign.

Scott keeps ship down to 800 feet all over this country, to avoid the wind at the higher levels. Our nose is down 10°, and the people on the ground probably think we are out of control and about to crash into the trees. It is wonderful what detail we see when flying at this low level. The trees each settler cut down last winter are neatly stacked, and look like little bundles of asparagus; and we see exactly where he gets his water, the extent of his housing accommodation, and the amount of land he has cultivated. The character of the soil is clearly visible to us, the natural drainage of the country stands revealed, and we get an insight into the rainfall, the types of trees which do best, the bird life and the depth of the lakes; whilst the glorious and invigorating fragrance of these enormous pine forests comes up to us as a refreshing tonic, putting new life into every one on board. We all agree we must come again to Nova Scotia for shooting and fishing.

8.40 *a.m.*—Following the St. Mary's Valley over the water-shed. Course W., twenty-one knots. Twenty-seven knots made good.

9.45 *a.m.*—Junction of Gayborough and Colchester counties, Nova Scotia.

We work out our speed over the ground to be twenty-seven knots by measuring shadow of Airship on the trees with stop-watch.

Shadow is one-tenth of a mile long.

12.30 *p.m.*—Lunch. The pine-saturated atmosphere has renewed every one's appetite. We are just getting into Fundy Bay. The petrol supply is distinctly serious. Shotter has been totalling up our available resources with ever-increasing anxiety.

We cannot now afford to run all five engines at once, as they would eat up too much petrol.

We have 500 miles yet to go to New York,

and if we don't get any wind or bad weather against us can do it all right on three engines, assisted occasionally by a fourth.

If we get much wind against us we are done, and will have to be taken in tow by a destroyer or other surface craft during the night (humiliating thought!)—the idea being that at dawn we would cast off and fly into Long Island under our own power.

Other alternatives are: (*a*) to come down to 300 feet, ride to our drogue (sea anchor) and take in petrol from a destroyer, or (*b*) to land at Boston, re-fuel there, and then proceed to New York.

A signal is sent through to the U.S. Naval Authorities at Washington and Boston asking them to send a destroyer to stand by to give us a tow should we need one. Hope it won't be necessary.[1]

It is now raining and foggy, which is the kind of weather that will suit us—fog and rain generally means no wind. Sea dead calm in the Bay.

---

[1] Afterwards we discovered that the W.T. Station at Bar Harbour had prefixed our message with the word "Rush," thus creating the unfortunate impression that R 34 was "in extremis"; whereas she was merely taking the precaution of asking a destroyer to meet her *in case* she should run short of petrol.

1.30 *p.m.*—We begin to notice distinct evidence of electrical disturbances.

2 *p.m.*—Though the sky has not got much worse, atmospherics have become very bad. Severe thunderstorm can be seen over New Brunswick, moving south down coast. This storm looks very large, and appears to be moving rapidly. Scott turns left-handed off his course towards Nova Scotia to avoid it, but storm also extends eastward. He puts on all engines to try and get away from it, and orders are given to stow away all loose valuables.

2.45 *p.m.*—Caught in violent squall on extreme outskirts of the storm. Ship very badly thrown about, rising 700 feet in one bump. We see these bumps or squalls passing over the water. They appear to be a line of circular squalls or " whirls " moving in line abreast at a very high speed. Storm almost tropical in its violence. Our first warning was when the helmsman pointed to the compass card, which was spinning round like a top.

Harris thinks that had we been caught in the centre of this storm, the bumps would have been so severe that the ship might have been damaged in the air.

Wonderful specimens of "Mammato Cumulus" cloud, indicating a highly perturbed state of the atmosphere. These clouds have a festoon-like appearance, and remind one rather of bunches of grapes—they are only associated with very severe disturbances. Photo by Pritchard. It is difficult to estimate the size of these storms, but as the squalls which hit the ship were about fifty miles from the storm itself, the area covered must have been many thousands of square miles.

During the summer months these storms are frequent on this coast, and are a grave danger to all aircraft. The U.S. Weather Bureau have made a special study of them, and are usually able to forecast them a considerable period before their breaking, as indeed they did upon this occasion.

3 *p.m.*—Crossing Haute Island—Fundy Bay—very pretty little island. Huge cliffs and lighthouse. Three-quarters covered with woods. Easterly cliff white with gulls. Started up third engine—only making good fifteen knots on two.

Unpleasant neuralgic toothache all down left side of face. Retired to hammock and took some aspirin. Hope not going to crock up.

3.45 *p.m.*—Message from United States Navy:

"Arrangements have been made for destroyers to be south of Cape Cod."

4 *p.m.*—"Destroyers *Bancroft* and *Stevens* left Boston to your assistance at 3.30 p.m.—Signed, Commander, 1st Naval District."

Shotter happened to be lying full length alongside drogue hatch when that last squall hit us and, when ship's nose first went down, would have slid through hatch into sea if he had not hooked a girder with his foot!

Feeling very tired, so turn in and sleep soundly, despite the creaking of the girders in the keel, and loud buffeting of the wind against the outer cover.

6 *p.m.*—Dodging another colossal thunderstorm. Had to haul in W.T. aerials, as attempts to use wireless resulted in two-inch sparks owing to highly charged atmosphere.

Ship again badly thrown about—very unusual temperature bumps. Come to the conclusion that a comfortable hammock is indeed the best place on occasions like these.

7.30 *p.m.*—We are well clear of Nova Scotia, and heading straight for New York. Making good twenty-four knots with three engines and slightly favourable wind. We again anxiously take stock of our petrol. If we don't get more than twelve miles wind against us from now on we can make New York on three engines, and if not more than fifteen against us, we can do it on two engines.

Particularly fine electrical disturbance sunset.

8 *p.m.*—Evening meal. Very hot, and our costumes are both scanty and varied. We discuss our prospects of getting straight through to New York. If we do not have any more of these electric storms we agree we have a good sporting chance.

9.20 *p.m.*—Durrant again lowers his aerials, but they charge up too quickly, and are at once reeled in.

9.30 *p.m.*—Violent temperature " bumps," evidently caused by rapid variation of sea temperature beneath us. Ship is first lifted 400 feet and then dropped 500 feet—measured on our aneroid. Scott, who has his head out of a window in the forward car, states that he saw the tail of the ship bend under the strain, whilst her angle is so steep at one moment that Cooke, resting in his hammock in the keel, is unable to get out for a minute or two, as he is head downwards at the time. Standing more out to sea, and running on all five engines to get further from this locality, a heartbreaking manœuvre,

OUTWARD JOURNEY

as it will reduce still further our depleted petrol supply. Harris has experienced something of this kind before, when aboard the s.s. *Montcalm* in these regions.[1] The sky was completely clear when the storm broke, wind practically calm, sea glassy, and moon brilliant. For a few seconds the warm air, which seemed pine scented (although we were well out to sea), was suddenly succeeded by very cold air, and it is these rapidly rising warm currents which throw the ship about with such violence.

Thunderstorms by day are bad enough, but at night they are particularly unpleasant, and the ship vibrates from bow to stern. We wear our parachutes, and life-belts are all ready.[2]

Our only bottle of brandy fell out of the chart locker with a crash during one of these vertical bumps—fortunately without breaking.

11.30 *p.m.*—Things now don't look at all well

[1] See footnote on p. 103.

[2] It is interesting to note that although these " temperature bumps " are the worst that any of us have yet experienced, the actual movements of the ship were felt by all to be quite slow and gradual; in fact, upon no single occasion has there been sufficient motion to cause the slightest sensation of sea-sickness. As Aerial liners undoubtedly will increase considerably in size, this immunity from sea-sickness should prove one of their most valuable commercial assets.

for our getting through to New York, and the following W.T. messages are sent and received.

Sunday, July 6th

12.10 *a.m.* G.M.T.—From R 34 to C.O., U.S. Naval Air Service, Chatham, Mass. : " If through shortage gasolene R 34 wishes to land Chatham can you supply 50,000 cubic feet hydrogen, and 500 gallons gasolene ? "

2.0 *a.m.*—From R 34 to C.O., U.S. Naval Air Service, Montauk, Long Island : " Can you land R 34 and give us 500 gallons gasolene—will arrive over Montauk 8 o'clock this morning ? "

2.50 *a.m.*—From U.S. Navy, Washington, to R 34 : " Advise 1st District immediately if you can. Facilities for landing have been provided."

3.30 *a.m.*—From U.S. Navy, Washington, to R 34 : " Personnel and material waiting at Mineola for instructions from you. Advise if you desire base elsewhere. Keep me informed of your movements.—Lucas."

3.50 *a.m.*—From R 34 to U.S. Navy, Washington : " Will land Montauk. Will report time later."

4.0 *a.m.*—U.S. Navy, Washington, to R 34 : " Arrangements being made to temporarily land

FIRST SIGHT OF LONG ISLAND.

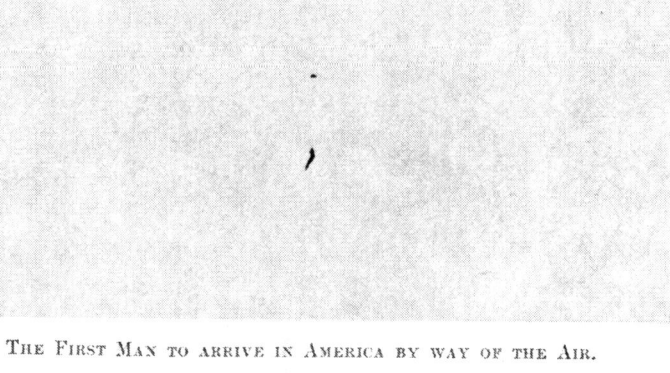

THE FIRST MAN TO ARRIVE IN AMERICA BY WAY OF THE AIR.

ship Montauk if it becomes essential. Keep us informed."

4.10 *a.m.*—Sight American soil at Chatham.

4.25 *a.m.*—S. end of Mahoney Island. The petrol situation has now become desperate, and Scott decides he must land at Montauk for petrol.

We all feel very disappointed, but it can't be helped.

5.30 *a.m.*—Passing over Martha's Vineyard, Massachusetts—a large island off the coast. Two biggish watering places—big hotels and many piers—evidently a yachting resort. Looks delightful.

Spoke American destroyer, who had come to help, and declined her assistance with thanks.

Interesting marble quarry on south side of island.

Wireless message from New York to R 34: "The American Flying Club cordially invite as guests of the A.F.C. the crew of R 34 during their stay in New York at the Hotel Commodore."

7.20 *a.m.*—Passing U.S. Naval Airship Station, Montauk, Long Island, with nice following wind. Our luck is in after all. We are making good speed and find we can just get right through to New York. What a relief!

We are now in touch with Mineola on our wireless telephony, and are told that Lieut. H. W. Hoyt, U.S.N., is on landing-ground ready to land us, but that Major Fuller has gone to Boston to land us there. Useful invention—wireless telephony, and quicker than wireless telegraphy.

As we skim over this American country-side, I confess to a delightful glow of satisfaction at gazing on American soil for the first time—from above. It brings home to me more than anything else could ever do, what a small place this world really is, what an astonishing part these great Airship Liners will play in linking together the remotest places of the earth; and what interesting years lie immediately ahead!

Lovely bungalows. All houses look quite different to English houses—so much more modern and of a different architectural style. Every house has a verandah, and they all seem to be built of wood.

8 *a.m.*—Breakfast; a hurried meal, for we all want to take in every detail of Long Island, which is slipping away beneath us. Lansdowne points out President Roosevelt's house at Oyster Bay, which looks charming from above. We should arrive at Hazelhurst Field, Mineola, our

OUTWARD JOURNEY

journey's end, by 10 o'clock. Suddenly remember that one might be " called upon to say a few words " after landing. Awful thought! Try and think out something of interest, but find it very difficult.

Am just beginning to realize that our exciting adventure is nearly over, and feel full of mixed feelings of pleasure and disappointment. There is one comforting thought, however—the prospect of the return journey.

9 *a.m.*—Great hustle and bustle on board! The keel is full of people struggling to close reluctant suit-cases, and to improve their generally dishevelled appearances—which takes a bit of doing. Thank goodness there are no bills to pay, or waiters to tip!

9.20 *a.m.*—Over Hazelhurst Field, admirably chosen by Major Fuller, whose excellent arrangements for landing us become plainly evident.[1] It is a bright, clear morning, and we can see a long line of motor-cars of every sort and size streaming out from New York to see us come

[1] Lt.-Col. F. W. Lucas, R.A.F., Major H. C. Fuller, R.A.F., Flt.-Sergts. Turner, Angus, and six airmen had come over to New York in advance to arrange for the landing, and it was largely owing to their efficiency and foresight that the ship was able to make such a successful return journey.

in. There is a large motor enclosure half a mile long, where cars are standing—already six deep. I find myself mechanically counting the rows—an enormous multitude of people are gazing up at us, and a military band is playing in front of a grand stand erected for the occasion.

As Major Fuller is away at Boston,[1] Pritchard volunteers to take his place, and descends by parachute for the purpose, Greenland and Luck helping him through the window of the forward car. After about 150 feet the parachute opens well, Pritchard makes a good landing, and can claim to be the first man to land in America by means of the air; whilst this episode shows another of those useful purposes to which parachutes may be put.

9.40 *a.m.*—Scott makes a complete circuit of the ground, carefully balances up his ship, and then—with perfect judgment—brings her down gently into the hands of the U.S. soldiers and sailors who form the landing-party.

Our actual time of landing is 9.54 a.m., or

[1] As it was thought at one time that we should be compelled to land at Boston, Major Fuller had motored to Boston to arrange for an emergency landing, accompanied by Commander Maxfield, U.S. Naval Air Service, and Capt. Craven, U.S.N., Director U.S. Naval Air Service.

A GROUP OF SOME OF THE OFFICERS AFTER LANDING IN AMERICA.

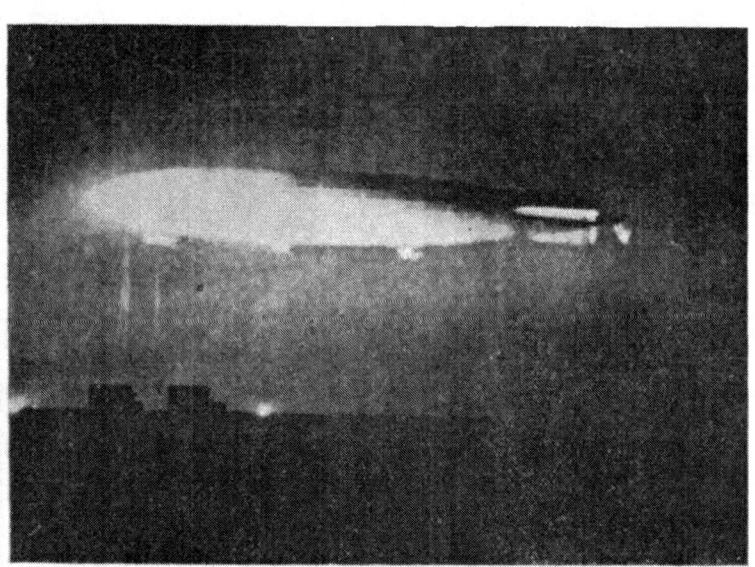

R 34 MOORED OUT AT MINEOLA. VIEWED BY SEARCHLIGHT.

OUTWARD JOURNEY

1.54 p.m. G.M.T.; and our total time for this outward journey from East Fortune to Mineola, New York, is 108 hours, 12 minutes.

We have 140 gallons of petrol left, or two hours at full speed, so we couldn't have cut it much finer, and are lucky indeed to get through!

OUR STAY IN AMERICA

Our Stay in America

As soon as the ship is made fast we clamber out of the forward car and are formally greeted by Vice-Admiral Gleaves, representing the United States Navy, and Major-General C. P. Menoher, Director U.S. Army Air Services.

The former makes a short speech, welcoming us as the first travellers to arrive by air on American soil, to which I briefly respond.

There are large numbers of American naval and military officers present; prominent amongst whom are Col. A. Miller, Commanding Military Aviation on Long Island, and Brig.-General Mitchell; also Lieuts. H. W. Hoyt, C. G. Little, J. J. Quinn, T. B. Null, and P. J. Barnes, A.F.C., all of the U.S. Naval Airship Service. These latter have been with us on convoy and anti-submarine duties off the east coast of England during the war—old friends whom we are glad to meet again. They prove of the greatest assistance, and take over the watch-keeping, refuelling and other responsible duties. It is entirely due to these and other officers and men of the United States Navy and Army that R 34 succeeded in mooring out so successfully during her stay in America.

Brig.-General L. E. O. Charlton, C.B., D.S.O., British Air Attaché, Washington, Lt.-Col. F. W. Lucas, Lt.-Col. Norman Thwaites, and Major J. Ogilvie Davis, are amongst the British representatives.

We talk with them for a few moments, and then are persuaded to give ourselves up for about fifteen minutes to the cinema operators and camera men. This is indeed a trying ordeal, and I shall never forget the "barrage" of cameras which confronted us! They were so numerous that the operators had to face us in two ranks—the front rank kneeling, and the rear rank standing behind!

This over, we have a much-needed wash and brush up, and then motor to the Garden City Hotel, where a wonderful banquet has been prepared for us by the United States Navy.

Vice-Admiral Gleaves, who presided, makes an excellent and amusing speech, and so does Lt.-Comdr. Read, pilot of N.C. 4 (who was the first man to fly the Atlantic, and whom I had last seen at the House of Commons, where he was being similarly entertained by Major-General Seeley, Under-Secretary of State for Air, after his Atlantic

OUR STAY IN AMERICA

crossing from west to east). Other speeches follow, and Scott, Cooke, Harris and myself each do our best in the speech-making line in so far as our oratorical talents and the cocktails would permit !

The following telegram is received from His Majesty the King, addressed to Officer Commanding H.M.A. R 34, Long Island —

"I am commanded by His Majesty to transmit the following message to you. Heartiest congratulations to yourself and crew of R 34 on your splendid achievement, and best wishes for a safe return. Your flight marks the beginning of an era in which the English-speaking peoples, already drawn together in war, will be even more closely united in peace.—F. H. SYKES."

The next two days are spent in paying official calls and exploring New York with General Charlton, whom I can never thank sufficiently for his many kindnesses; also lunching and dining with friends—both new and old. The United States Navy very kindly place a suite of rooms at the Ritz-Carlton at our disposal, also some motor-cars, and we are overwhelmed with hospitality on every side. The dentist whom I visit in Fifth Avenue repudiates any suggestion of a fee (an autograph is accepted in lieu), and this is merely one example of the generous hospitality we receive everywhere. We thought America had " gone dry," but are quickly undeceived upon this point!

Finally, on Wednesday evening President Wilson, having himself only arrived that same afternoon from Europe, did us the honour of congratulating us in the Town Hall, and invited us on to the platform, while he made one of his most important speeches on the state of affairs in Europe.

During these three days the Airship has been moored out in the open on the landing-ground at Mineola, and the following extracts from Major Scott's report best describe the conditions that were experienced.

Mooring R 34 at Mineola.—The system employed was the free three-wire system, where all three wires are brought to a common ring in the centre on the ground.

During the day it was the custom to haul the ship down and hold by man power, so that the necessary work on engines, etc., could be carried out.

At night she would be let up into the air about 150 feet with nobody on board.

Attached is a rough log giving details during the mooring—

July 6th.—Landed at 9.54 a.m.

OUR STAY IN AMERICA

Landing-party holding ship during morning and afternoon, filling up with water ballast as ship heats up.

4 *p.m.*—Thunderstorm passed, accompanied by heavy rain. All water ballast was released, but ship was still so heavy that after car could not be raised off the ground, with the result that all handling rails on after car were carried away.[1]

Commenced gassing at once, but ship not light enough to let up on moorings until 10.0 p.m., when she was let up 150 feet into the air and landing-party released.

July 7th.—During the night rain dried off, and a hot sun coming out in the morning, the ship becomes so light that hauling down is very difficult.

During this operation, the casting in the hull right forward (where the mooring-point is attached) pulled out. Fortunately the casting jammed in the shackle, or the ship might have broken away altogether.

During the day the mooring-point forward is stiffened up with timber and wire strops, so that, in the evening, Scott is able to let her up once more.

The trim of the ship is much better this time, and she rides 4° down by the stern.

---

[1] This will be prevented on future occasions by the use of special handling cages, as used in Germany.

July 8th.—During the night ship tended to become heavy; but it was found possible, with the assistance of about thirty men, to haul her tail down sufficiently to allow a man to climb aboard the after car. He then proceeded up into the keel, and let go water ballast. This operation was performed twice.

She was again hauled down during the day, special visitors being allowed aboard, and subsequently let up for the night.

July 9th.—The weather forecasts are now more suitable for the homeward journey. It was decided, therefore, to leave late that night or early next morning.

During the day the wind got up considerably, and became very gusty, two very nasty squalls just missing the ship. In consequence, it was decided to get away on our return journey at the earliest possible moment, and gassing operations were started as soon as the sun went down.

When actually at her moorings, R 34 rode easily and behaved in a very satisfactory manner; and this experience at Mineola goes far to demonstrate that the larger the ship the less difficult will be the mooring-out problems.

It also showed that the three-wire system is quite useful as an emergency method of mooring.

HOMEWARD JOURNEY

LONG ISLAND—NEW YORK TO PULHAM, NORFOLK

WEDNESDAY, JULY 9TH

Time 11.30 *p.m.* (*New York summer time.*)—It is very dark, and the wind is gusting up to thirty miles an hour on the ground.

Our final preparations are made in the ghostly light of powerful searchlights, which are concentrated on the ship both fore and aft, clearly showing up the United States soldiers who form the handling party. Gas, petrol, water—everything is safely on board—including food for the return journey.

We have made hosts of friends during our three wonderful days in America, and they are all here on the ground to see us off.

11.40 *p.m.*—Last farewells. Crew are all aboard, and Scott releases ballast to ensure the ship being light when starting. At the last moment another bag of mails and a case of rum are thrown in through the open window of the forward car.

11.54 p.m. (*July 9th, New York summer time, or 3.54 a.m., July 10th, Greenwich mean time*).—Away.

A great cheer comes up to us as we rise into the sky and steer straight for New York, having promised to fly over the city before heading out into the Atlantic.

Again that strange feeling of loneliness—as sudden as it is transient. Scott has 4500 gallons of petrol on board; this should be ample and to spare for the return journey, which we anticipate will be nothing like so difficult as our journey over. Taking into account the gusty wind, and difficult conditions generally on the landing ground, and the fact that Scott was unable to get an opportunity of ballasting up his ship, it is an extremely good "get-away." Our trim is only 3° down by the stern, and the prospects for a successful journey are quite satisfactory.

The disposable weights for this return journey are as follows—

	Weight
Petrol, 4500 gallons	14·43 tons
Oil, 230 gallons	·95 ,,
Water (including drinking), 800 gallons	3·57 ,,
Crew, food, clothing, etc.	4·00 ,,
Spares	·25 ,,
Total weight	23·20 tons.

THURSDAY, JULY 10TH

New York at night looks wonderful from a height of 1000 feet—miles and miles of tiny bright twinkling lights.

We wonder if it is necessary to go higher than 1000 feet to avoid bumping into the "skyscrapers," so Scott puts her up to 1500 feet to be quite sure!

The searchlights at first make some very unsuccessful attempts to find us, and their beams are " feeling " through the sky in every direction.

Finally they get us fair and square over Fifth Avenue.

The Times Square, Broadway, is a remarkable sight—we see thousands of upturned faces in spite of the early hour (1 a.m.), and the whole scene is lit up by the gigantic electrical sky-signs, which seem to concentrate about this point. One in particular—the Overland car—is a fine example of the importance of aerial advertisement, and from a height of 2000 feet we can see its wheels revolving, and the dust rising in clouds behind it, presumably as an illustration of its speed.

The air over New York feels very disturbed,

partly owing to the approaching cyclone from the Great Lakes, of which we have already had warning, and partly also to the heat rising upwards from the city itself; in spite of this the ship is very steady.

1.10 *a.m.* (*New York, summer time*).—We head for home with 3000 miles of sea between us and our Scottish base.

The wind is now well behind, and our speed made good is estimated to be sixty-five knots, or seventy-eight miles an hour.

The weather at time of starting is decidedly helpful for a flight from America to England.

There is a depression west of Newfoundland, and another larger one centred to the north of Iceland; also an anti-cyclone over the Eastern Atlantic and Great Britain.

The inference from the above is that a strong S.W. or W. wind will prevail over the greater part of the Atlantic, and, being on the southerly side of the depression centred over Newfoundland, we should get the full benefit of the thirty-five-knot S.W. wind which is blowing.

At this speed (seventy-eight miles an hour) we are travelling considerably faster than the depression itself, which is probably moving eastwards at about thirty-five knots, or 42 m.p.h., and it

HOMEWARD JOURNEY

may well be that we shall run right out of it before we reach mid-Atlantic.

With any luck, by keeping rather northerly of the steamship course, we may get into touch with the still bigger depression centred to the north of Iceland, and so benefit by the westerly wind which we ought to find on its southerly side.

2.17 *a.m.*—Our course is now east 49°, and we are crossing the American coast six miles east of Bellport, with four of our five engines running, the fifth engine resting.—Very dark night.

Some hot coffee from the Thermos flasks presented to us by kind American friends is particularly nice and warming.

Decide to turn in.

5.10 *a.m.*—Nantucket light-ship bears northeast of us, distance five miles.

9.15 *a.m.*—We have covered 430 miles from New York already, and are going strong. After breakfast Scott and I sort out the mails, and this takes some time, as we find we have quite a large collection of parcels and letters of all descriptions. There are letters for H.M. the King, the Foreign Office, Admiralty, Postmaster-General; and a large number of copies of the *Public Ledger* for the editor of *The Times*.

In addition we have cinematograph films of

our landing in America, President Wilson's reception in New York, the Dempsey-Willard fight, and also medals for Alcock and Brown presented by the Aero Club of America.

This journey, we hope, will prove to be the fastest newspaper delivery between New York and London yet accomplished, and will be the forerunner of a regular interchange of mails between East and West.

10.45 *a.m.*—We are now making good seventy-two knots or 86 m.p.h. on four engines—forward engine stopped.

Wind almost dead astern, and very little drift.

Have consultation with Scott, and we decide to make straight for London and see how long it will take to cross the Atlantic from Broadway to Piccadilly Circus; from the capital of one country to the capital of the other. Cooke asleep under the dining-room table; this looks bad, and reminds one of the tales about one's ancestors—but there is no cause for anxiety!

12 *noon.*—Lunch. Cold Bologna sausage and pickles, stewed pineapple and a ration of rum. This latter is much appreciated, as the weather has turned much colder.

We discuss at some length the problem of obtaining and recording meteorological information about the upper air in the Atlantic, and all agree that one good method of getting information at small cost would be to equip all cable repair-ships with a meteorological observer, and a suitable outfit of kites and instruments.

These cable repair-ships work in all parts of the world, and are often stationary at sea for days at a time; moreover, the cable routes are nearly in every case on the shortest and most direct routes between the countries they link up.[1]

We send following messages via Bar Harbour to Admiral Commanding Naval District, Mineola—

" Officers and crew R 34 desire to express their sincere gratitude for the valuable and efficient assistance they have received during the mooring out of R 34 at Mineola. All well—making good progress. Distance covered 630 miles in twelve hours—making for London.—SCOTT."

To Colonel Miller, Long Island—

" Officers and crew R 34 thank you personally

---

[1] Harris, just previous to this flight, had been carrying out meteorological investigations for the Air Ministry from the s.s. *Montcalm* in this part of the Atlantic, and his experience shows that kites can be flown at 2000 feet in winds from ten to seventy-five miles per hour (hurricane force) without damage to kite or instrument. The instrument used is a Marvin meteograph, which records force of wind, altitude, temperature and humidity, and can be run up to the kite and back again as required without having to haul down.

for trouble you have taken to help us while moored out—it is much appreciated.—Going strong for London—distance covered in twelve hours, 630 miles.—SCOTT."

1.5 *p.m.*—We have averaged 67 m.p.h. ever since leaving New York.

Weather fine—visibility fifteen to twenty miles—wind forty knots, S.S.W.—sea very rough.

It is difficult to measure the height of waves from above, but it is easy to see that, in a very heavy sea like this, a surface ship would be having an extremely bad time. Up here we are as steady as a rock, and unless we look out of the windows, it is hard to realize we are travelling at all.

The sun is high, so Cooke is able to get good idea of any barometric changes by observing the angle the ship's shadow on the water subtends with a sextant, thus calculating the distance of the shadow from the observer, and comparing with height recorded on the altimeter. This is only possible at low altitudes, *i.e.* about 1500 feet. (It sounds a bit complicated, but is quite effective!) Lt.-Col. W. N. Hensley, United States Army Aviation Department, is steering, and is taking opposite watch with Pritchard, while Luck has relieved Greenland in the forward car, and

CLOUD SHADOWS THROWN UPON THE ATLANTIC.

INTERIOR OF R 34, SHOWING WALKING-WAY AND
PETROL TANKS. TAKEN ON BOARD DURING FLIGHT.

Warrant-Officer Mayes is in charge of the elevators.

Course direct for London via Queenstown and Bristol Channel. We are in wireless touch with Sable Island, and about 300 miles due south of Newfoundland.

2 *p.m.*—Received the following two wireless messages from New York—

" To R 34 : Thanks for the flight, from thousands whom the spectacle thrilled—good luck to you.—*New York Times.*"

" God speed you on return to England. Hope your voyage is only forerunner of many.—*New York Herald.*"

We report our progress as follows—

" To Air Attaché, Washington, Air Ministry and Base, via New York. Course 90 true—speed 50 knots—going well."

U.S. Weather Bureau warn us that weather is very bad over Newfoundland, and advise us to keep as much away to the south as possible.

Harris estimates we shall have got away from the influence of this depression by nightfall, and that probably the wind and sea will have moderated by then. There is still the possibility of getting into touch with the depression centred over Iceland by (about) to-morrow afternoon. As a general rule it is foggy and cloudy the more we keep up to the north, the cold currents, meeting the warm currents, causing fog and cloud. On a more southerly course over the Gulf Stream, where there are no cold currents from the north, clearer weather can always be expected.

4.50 *p.m.*—Position 42° 15′ N., 54° 05′ W., determined by observations of sun to sea horizon.[1] True bearing sun N. 81° W. Course 140° steered, 110° made good, speed 57 m.p.h. We have covered 900 miles from New York in sixteen hours, and are 1850 miles from S. coast of Ireland, or exactly one-third of the distance between the two countries.

Our petrol consumption works out at about one gallon an hour on four engines—weather clear. Our maximum visibility is very good and, according to the Dip and Distance horizon tables, at our present height, *i. e.* 1500 ft., should be about forty-five miles. Wind has dropped considerably, and sea is deep blue.

It is interesting to note that, with depressions situated as they are, it would be quite against all

[1] There were only three occasions on the outward journey when it was possible to determine our position by means of observations of sun to sea horizon.

HOMEWARD JOURNEY

the laws of weather forecasting for us to get a head wind anywhere between here and London. The worst condition that we might expect to get would be no wind at all.

Wireless message to U.S. Weather Bureau—

"Many thanks for kind, efficient manner in which weather information has been supplied—deeply grateful.—GUY HARRIS, Meteorological Officer, R 34."

6.15 *p.m.*—A five-masted schooner under full sail on starboard beam about five miles away—the first ship we have yet seen in the open Atlantic on either outward or return journeys.

What an interesting contrast between the old and the new—the sailing ship and the airship! We are now over the main eastbound summer route of steamers from New York to Queenstown, so perhaps we may meet an outward-bound liner.

The s.s. *Adriatic*, due New York on 13th, should be somewhere near us, and we are on the look-out for her on our wireless.

Getting much colder as we go further east.

7.30 *p.m.*—Harris gives most interesting explanation of the cloud formations to the north and south, and compares the clouds as we see them with the illustrations in Claydon's book on *Cloud Studies* which we have on board.

8 *p.m.*—Supper-time—fresh boiled eggs and cocoa, preceded by a cocktail mixed by Scott. Apparently some Thermos flasks full of cocktail ingredients had been handed in by some anonymous well-wisher, and we try them as an experiment. Decide that they are just as good in the air as on the ground!

We compare at some length our impressions of American men and women. I wish our newly-made American friends could have heard some of the delightful things that were said about them.[1]

8.30 *p.m.*—Pritchard goes to sleep under the dining-room table while the second watch come in for their supper. This position (under the dining-room table) seems to be the most sought after in the ship!

The gramophone is a real pleasure on this homeward journey; a magnificent instrument presented to Scott by Mr. Edison.

One of our pigeons escaped at Mineola when allowed out for exercise,[2] and so we have only one

---

[1] Quite a number of charming ladies declared their intention of making the return journey as " stowaways," and the ship was carefully searched before starting.

[2] This pigeon was afterwards picked up in an exhausted condition by a west-bound steamer 800 miles out in the Atlantic having made a most valiant attempt to fly back to England.

on the return journey. He takes his food well, and " coos " loudly every time the gramophone starts up—his wicker cage being hung on a girder just outside the crew's mess-deck.

L.A.C. Graham was offered 1000 dollars for his cat in America just before leaving, but said indignantly that he would not consider 5000 dollars, or any other sum!

11.58 p.m.—British ship s.s. *Minnekahda* speaks us. She says she is bound for Halifax with troops. During this first day in the Atlantic the sea has been visible the whole time, so that observations for course and speed have been obtained as often as necessary and without any difficulty.

Friday, July 11th

3.20 a.m.—Position 45° 03′ N., 42° 57′ W., estimated by observations of stars to sea horizon.

4.20 a.m.—The foremost of the two engines in after car is out of action : damaged beyond repair.[1] Scott and myself discuss the situation, and agree we had better make straight for our base at East Fortune, and give up the idea of flying in over London.

[1] The cause of this breakdown turned out to be accidental declutching whilst under load, allowing the engine to race. For some unexplained reason the governor gear failed to operate.

We change course accordingly, and are now making good N. 30° E.; weather clear—sea moderate.

6.40 *a.m.*—Scott brings ship down to the 600-foot level, to get under clouds which are now appearing, and threaten to blot out all view of the sea.

We find by careful observation that there is a northerly wind below the clouds, whilst above, on the 3000-foot level, the wind is from the S.W.

The reason for this is interesting: we are over the Gulf Stream on a north-easterly course, and the air over this Gulf Stream is warmer than the air over the sea immediately to the north. This warm air rises, and its place is naturally taken by the cold air from the north, resulting in a twelve-knot convectional wind extending from the surface of the sea up to a height of about 2000 feet.

Having made this discovery, we remain at the 3000-foot level above the clouds, where we have a steady wind from the S.W.

We find it easy to determine the direction of wind, when flying above clouds, from their formation. The crests of these curl over away from the direction in which the wind is blowing.

HOMEWARD JOURNEY

9.15 *a.m.*—Clocks have been put forward one hour.

10.30 *a.m.*—Scott and Harris are agreed that the wind is stronger in our favour the higher we go up. In spite of this Scott decides to remain on the 3000-foot level to avoid necessity of losing gas from expansion.

To-morrow he can afford to go much higher, as the ship will be so much lighter, on account of having burnt another twenty-four hours' petrol. Beautiful cloudscapes on port beam. Cloud formations, in so far as they indicate weather, are like an open book profusely illustrated, and with a story that changes almost completely every few hours.

Away to the N.W. we see the depression centred over Newfoundland written plainly in the sky, in fantastic and streaky " Cirrus ventosus "— a sure indication of what is going on over there, some hundreds of miles away.

12 *noon.*—Weather report from Air Ministry tells us of an anti-cyclone off S.W. of Ireland, and so we change course more to the north, with a view to getting round into the westerly wind, which we know must be blowing on the northerly side of it. Noon position, 46° 31′ N., 38° 32′ W.

Still above the clouds. Cooke considers the best height at which to take sights to cloud horizon is at about 500 feet above the clouds.

12.30 *p.m.*—Lunch. Meal-times are always most welcome, as they give the more responsible members of the crew a much-needed interval.

The new gramophone is going strong after lunch and, as I was descending the ladder into the forward car, I caught a glimpse of Luck and Harris doing quite a nice one-step together!

12.45 *p.m.*—Speak s.s. *San Florino* bound for Tampico, Gulf of Mexico, from Southampton.

1.30 *p.m.*—Air Ministry send message to say they have made provision to land us in Ireland if necessary, and that destroyers with steam up are available at Berehaven if required. We reply, " Propose to land at East Fortune—one engine completely broken down."

Message from New York—

" At this luncheon given by Aero Club of America resolutions were passed to the effect that the officers and officials of the Club wish General Maitland and crew of R 34 safe and pleasant journey.—LUCAS."

Big glare off the clouds—very noticeable coming down from keel into the forward car.

HOMEWARD JOURNEY

Harris and Cooke climb to top of ship to make observations every two hours; quite a strenuous effort each time, and they at any rate cannot complain for want of exercise.

3.30 *p.m.*—Still at 3000 feet; in and out of the clouds at intervals. We have not seen the sea since 8.30 a.m. this morning. Air speed thirty-two knots on three engines. Another weather report from London to say that the depression N. of Iceland has moved easterly, and that, as a result, the wind is from S.W. over north of Ireland, and whole of Scotland. This strengthens Scott in his decision to give up going to London, and to make East Fortune instead.

It is sad not to take in London on our return route, but with one engine lost, and wind in S. of England not very favourable, the decision is a wise one.

4.30 *p.m.*—Scott brings his ship down to try for a glimpse of the sea, and so get an idea of our speed; but at 900 feet it is still quite thick, and so he abandons the attempt.[1]

Coming down from the 3800-foot level to the

[1] We need an instrument for measuring the depth of the clouds below an airship without having to reduce height for the purpose; probably a "Dines" or a "Marvin" kite meteograph would be suitable.

900-foot level, we pass through no less than five distinct and separate layers of cloud, of which every two layers contain a world in themselves, with separate sky above and cloud horizon beneath. A most fascinating spectacle, and one which impresses me more, perhaps, than anything I have yet seen on either journey.

We have been in these thick clouds for some considerable time, and there is no means of telling our speed, as they extend right down to the surface of the water.

We assume, however, from general weather observations, that the wind is with us; the worst condition we think fair to assume being no wind at all. There certainly ought *not* to be a head-wind against us. No alternative but to keep plugging away through these clouds until other weather conditions appear.

4.45 *p.m.*—We emerge above the clouds for a few blissful moments, and see a beautiful cloud panorama—range upon range of alternate white and slate coloured mountains with wide deep valleys, and an occasional glimpse of bright blue sky immediately above.

The glare is almost blinding, and we can only look at them for a moment or two at a time.

HOMEWARD JOURNEY

5 *p.m.*—Back again in the clouds, and no visibility whatsoever.

We pick up H.M.S. *Cumberland* on our Marconi spark set. She gives her position and, when plotted on chart, Cooke thinks she should be almost due north of us and, from the strength of her signals, within thirty miles.

Durrant tries to get her on the Directional Wireless, but without success.

Scott makes the discovery that when he brings his ship down into a cloud she will sometimes tend to dive, and at others tend to climb out of the cloud.

Pritchard puts forward the following interesting solution, which seems to fulfil the conditions each time it is observed.

" If a cloud is forming, the water vapour in the atmosphere is condensing, and giving off heat to the air during the process. The air, therefore, in a cloud which is forming is slightly warmer than the air immediately above the cloud. The Airship would, therefore, appear to be heavy and tend to dive on entering the cloud.

" If, on the other hand, the cloud is dissipating, the water in the cloud is evaporating and taking heat from the air in the cloud in doing so.

The air in the cloud is, therefore, colder than the air immediately above the cloud, and the Airship on entering the cloud will appear to be light."

7.5 *p.m.*—Passing through wet rain clouds—it has been raining very heavily since five o'clock.

Scott tries the 5000-foot level in the hopes of getting out of it, but with no success, so returns to the 3000-foot level. Very cold and dark, and all doors and windows shut.

Stopped forward engine to replace two broken valve-springs.

7.35 *p.m.*—We ask H.M.S. *Cumberland* for a weather report. She replies, giving her position, and reports : " Wind N.N.W.—18 m.p.h.—overcast—passing showers—clouds at about 1000 feet."

8 *p.m.*—Supper, and a very good one too. We are well equipped with little luxuries, having learnt from experience on the outward journey exactly what is necessary and what isn't.

Delicious fresh honey, also " candies," and chocolates supplied by Sherry's. The gloom does not affect our appetites in the very slightest.

8.30 *p.m.*—Still pouring in sheets. The wind whistles round the forward car, and it is very dark and dreary—of course we can see nothing.

Scott tries a lower level, and an extraordinary

HOMEWARD JOURNEY 117

sight immediately presents itself beneath us. Thousands and thousands of little round clouds like tiny white puff-balls packed closely together, with the blue sea just visible in between them, forming a layer of clouds between us and the sea. This cloud formation is known as " Ball cumulus," and is particularly beautiful. Harris has never seen " Ball cumulus " so low before; it is usually found at much greater heights.

8.45 *p.m.*—Dropped a calcium flare,[1] which floated away straight astern, burning brightly, enabling Cooke to get an estimate of course made good. Our speed is evidently considerable, but as no means exists of taking an angle of depression of the flare, it cannot be calculated.

In future we must be equipped with some instrument or other for this purpose.

8.50 *p.m.*—Again in thick cloud and heavy rain. Signals from Clifden Wireless Station sound very

[1] Flares for use at night are an absolute necessity, and the ones we use are the calcium phosphate flares commonly known in the Navy and Merchant Service as " Holmes " Lights. They will not float in rough weather, and so we attach to each flare a small fabric bag, which can be blown up with air by means of the mouth. Though a clumsy arrangement, it functions well; but, in future, we must have these " Holmes " Lights fitted with a watertight compartment to make certain of their floating in any sea.

loud, which shows we are getting nearer home, and Durrant has just succeeded in getting East Fortune (over 1600 miles away). Quite faintly he got the words, " Saturday evening."

9.15 *p.m.*—s.s. *Dominion*, bound for Avonmouth, speaks us and gives her position and barometer reading. She reports us as quite near, though of course she cannot see or even hear us.

10 *p.m.*—Speaking s.s. *Orduna*.

It is one thing talking to these ships in the Atlantic miles and miles away; but if only we could see them, how much nicer it would be.

11.25 *p.m.*—From s.s. *Dominion* : "Shall I fire a gun when I think you are near me? Estimate your speed at 45 m.p.h.—CHRISTIE."

We reply, " No, don't trouble to fire a gun."

On long journeys like these, it is the engineers upon whom the heaviest strain falls and, on the outward journey, some of them had difficulty in sleeping when off watch. On this return journey we issue them a " tot " of rum before turning in, with very beneficial effect.

12 *midnight.*—Still pouring with rain; by dropping two more flares drift is estimated to be 10° to southward. Height 2000 feet. Rain is beating down pitilessly against the outer cover, and the

whistling of the wind completely deadens the distant hum of our engines. It is indeed a " dirty " night at sea. For some reason or other I cannot get off to sleep, and lie awake in my hammock with a feeling of complete confidence and security, but hoping it won't be like this for our landing in Scotland to-morrow evening.

SATURDAY, JULY 12TH

12.45 *a.m.*—Weather clearing, and sea visible at 2500 feet.

5 *a.m.*—Magnificent sunrise; the sun slowly appears above the cloudbank ahead of us in a blaze of golden light, and we head straight into it.

6 *a.m.*—Position 52° 20′ N., 22° 35′ W., observation of sun to cloud horizon; 760 miles from East Fortune.

Running on three engines only; changing broken valve-spring on after engine. Air speed thirty-two knots; Scott takes ship down to 900 feet to sight the water. As speed made good at this height is only fifteen knots, however, he returns to 2800 feet, the surface being now just visible at this height, and speed made good increases to thirty-six knots.

It is interesting to note that for twenty-four hours (until 6 a.m. this morning) Cooke has been unable to get a single observation on either sun, moon, stars, sea or cloud horizons, and it is quite fair to assume that yesterday's weather is an average day in mid-Atlantic.

7 *a.m.*—Clouds beneath us look just like a soft, fleecy, white feather-bed, and they fill one with an odd, almost irresistible wish to jump down into them—probably the same sort of sensation experienced by some people when crossing a steep mountain face.

8 *a.m.*—H.M.S. *Tiger* gives her position, and reports: " Wind N.W.N., 15–20 m.p.h.—sky overcast with low stratus; visibility five miles."

We appear to have a slight head wind, but don't think it will last long, as we should soon be getting a helping wind from the depression over Scotland.

8.30 *a.m.*—Breakfast this morning is a festive meal, as we reckon it should be our last breakfast on board, and we are rather lavish in our issues.

East Fortune report weather suitable for a landing up till 8 a.m. to-morrow (Sunday) morning.

10 a.m.—We speak s.s. *Masirah*—she gives her position as Lat. 53° 30′ N., and Long. 18° 10′ W.

Signal from Air Ministry instructing us to land at Pulham in Norfolk. This is not understood as, according to weather reports, conditions seem to be better at East Fortune than at Pulham. Besides, the wives, families and sweethearts of the crew are all at East Fortune, waiting to welcome them, so to most of them this comes as a great disappointment.

10.40 a.m.—Drift observation obtained from about 3000 feet, and steering course is altered to N. 75° E., giving course made good N. 88° E. magnetic.

10.55 a.m.—Height 5000 feet. We are now over a big gap in the clouds, about twenty miles across. Clear blue sky and sea—making good thirty-five knots, which should enable us to land at daybreak to-morrow.

11.10 a.m.—Wireless message from Fermoy: "Do you intend to land at Fermoy? for I have landing-party of 500 men if required.—MAJOR LITTLE." [1]

---

[1] Major Little is one of our most experienced airship captains, and has been sent over to Ireland to land us at Fermoy Barracks, in the event of our running short of petrol.

We reply, " No, not landing at Fermoy."

We have a large supply of petrol left, and so far this journey has not presented half the difficulties of the outward voyage.

11.25 *a.m.*—Durrant succeeds in getting a cut on Clifden with directional finding apparatus.

Weather now very cold.

12 *noon.*—Lunch. We are becoming rather impatient to get to our journey's end. Perhaps it is the strain that is beginning to tell; anyway we all feel disappointed at finding we are only making good twenty-eight knots, and that there is quite a stiff north-easterly breeze against us. We shall be breakfasting in the air again to-morrow after all!

There must be a considerable amount of strain upon the entire crew during a flight of this kind, which is not felt consciously at the time, but shows itself in many little ways, such as the intense feeling sometimes displayed over very trivial matters.

There is little doubt that a crew doing a lot of long-distance journeys would in time suffer from some form of nerves, unless given a considerable amount of leave.

12.30 *p.m.*—The clouds have all cleared away; but only temporarily, I feel certain.

HOMEWARD JOURNEY

We are on the 5000-foot level, with a perfectly clear blue sky and deep blue sea; visibility is at its maximum, and at this height, according to our text-books, we should be able to see a distance of eighty-one miles from right forward to right aft, yet—although this area of visibility works out at 19,200 square miles—not a ship is in sight. I am afraid that my ambition to see a steamer at close quarters in this gigantic Atlantic will never be realized. If it wasn't for the fact that we have been actually speaking to them all the way across, I should feel inclined to say there are none in the Atlantic at all.

2.12 *p.m.*—Intercept message from East Fortune to Airship SSZ.75 instructing her to " drop pamphlets over Coast Towns." [1]

3.50 *p.m.*—Clouds rolling up again. We see some very fine examples of " Cumulus major." There is one particularly interesting cloudscape on our port beam—a huge vertical column about 500 feet high, joining a lower strata of cloud to a higher strata. This is caused by an upward vertical current, and beyond its picturesque effect has no special meaning.

[1] Presumably the pamphlets are to urge the public to buy War Loan.

5.30 *p.m.*—Great excitement; two trawlers are sighted on our starboard beam, about eight miles away, and looking very tiny—one is much nearer than the other. We try and speak the near one with an Aldis lamp, as they carry no wireless, but can get no reply. We are now down to 2000 feet, and the difference in temperature between this height and 5000 feet is most marked, viz. 8° F.

Making slightly better headway at this height, viz. thirty-two knots on four engines—wind N.N.W., 25° drift. Discussion with Cooke on subject of Aerial Navigation. He thinks that this should not present any insuperable difficulties; and that, with instruments at present available, one should be able to estimate one's position in mid-Atlantic accurately to within forty miles. Artificial horizons cannot be relied upon, owing to the necessity of keeping the reflected image continually in sight; and this difficulty is accentuated from a constantly moving platform like an Airship, however steady she may be. Until Directional Wireless proves thoroughly reliable a Bubble Sextant should be specially designed, and probably could be made to give an accuracy within about ten miles. It is extraordinary how

HOMEWARD JOURNEY

seldom we get a view of the sea. On the outward voyage, out of seventeen sights taken with the ordinary sextant, in three cases only was a sea horizon used—for the remaining fourteen the altitude was measured to a cloud horizon. On this return voyage it is slightly better and, so far, about half the sights taken have been to a sea horizon.

6.50 *p.m.*—We run into a sudden squall from the N.W., low black clouds with pelting rain and a rough confused sea; the wind roars past the control car. All this comes upon us in the space of a few minutes. Ship very steady.

6.57 *p.m.*—Passed out of squall. There appear to be more ahead. Got Clifden on Directional Wireless N. 98° E., Magnetic 76° true, and we cannot be very far from the west coast of Ireland. The clock is put on another hour.

7.15 *p.m.*—Another squall strikes us just as suddenly as the last one.

7.25 *p.m.*—Land in sight on our starboard bow; it is from seven to ten miles away, and was first spotted by Lt.-Col. Hensley. Great enthusiasm. Scott alters course direct towards it—Cooke gets out the large chart of the west coast of Ireland, and we have a keen competition to see who will fix on the exact spot where we cross the coast-line.

7.30 *p.m.*—Two little islands lie right ahead of us; with our glasses we see the wireless masts at Clifden. These two islands are undoubtedly the same two little islands that suddenly appeared out of the fog to the delighted gaze of Alcock and Brown upon the conclusion of their historical flight. What a strange and happy coincidence!

8 *p.m.*—At 8 o'clock precisely we cross the coast-line a little to the north of Clifden, County Mayo, and our time from crossing the American coast at Long Island to crossing the Irish coast is exactly 61 hours, 43 minutes.

8.15 *p.m.*—We head right in over the mountains, which at this spot are 2900 feet high. What a wild and rugged coast-line! A magnificent cloud panorama now appears—huge white cumulus clouds of weird and fantastic shapes surround us on all sides. Over the top peep out the mountain summits while, through gaps in the clouds, we catch glimpses of lakes, harbours, islands and green fields; quite the prettiest picture we have seen on the entire voyage. It seems as if the elements had reserved their best cloudscapes to welcome us as we cross over Irish soil.

LOW-LYING CUMULUS CLOUDS.

ABOVE THE HILLS AND LAKES OF NORTH IRELAND.

9.10 *p.m.*—A two-seater aeroplane from the neighbourhood of Castlebar flies successively past, over, and under us, waving a welcome. We are now well away from the mountains, and over the flat country inland, heading across to Belfast, and making good 46 m.p.h. Bright full moon.

As things have turned out, it would have been wiser if we had kept a more northerly course, after getting away from the helpful influence of the Newfoundland depression. We would then have been helped, instead of hindered, by this N.N.W. wind, and so have saved time. Undoubtedly the captains of future Airship Liners will become wily and cunning masters of the art of selecting the right wind and the right height, and, by means of their air knowledge alone, will save many hours upon long sea and land passages.

11.30 *p.m.*—Another message from Air Ministry to say we are to land at Pulham; we ask if we may land at East Fortune, as that was our original objective, and the weather is reported good for landing. The reply is to land at Pulham; so we assume there is some special reason, and alter course accordingly. Scott increases height to 5000 feet, and sets course direct for Pulham.

Turn in. We shall need a good night's rest,

as to-morrow is likely to be a very tiring day—to say the least of it.

Sunday, July 13th

2.45 *a.m.*—Flying up the Mersey. On our port bow are the lights of Liverpool. We are continually in and out of dense cloud banks, and it is difficult to identify places on the ground through occasional holes in the cloud strata beneath.

4.20 *a.m.*—Over Nottingham.

Wireless message from His Majesty the King: " I heartily congratulate you all on your safe return home after the completion of your memorable and indeed unique Atlantic voyage.—GEORGE, R.I."

4.40 *a.m.*—From Air Ministry to General Maitland, Major Scott, officers and crew of R 34: " On behalf of the whole Air Force I send you heartiest congratulations on your magnificent achievement in making the double journey across the Atlantic.—TRENCHARD, Chief of Air Staff."

4.46 *a.m.*—From Board of Admiralty to General Maitland and crew of H.M.A. R 34: " Welcome home. The great adventure of R 34 is beyond all praise.—Board of Admiralty."

5 *a.m.*—From Major-General Seeley, Under-

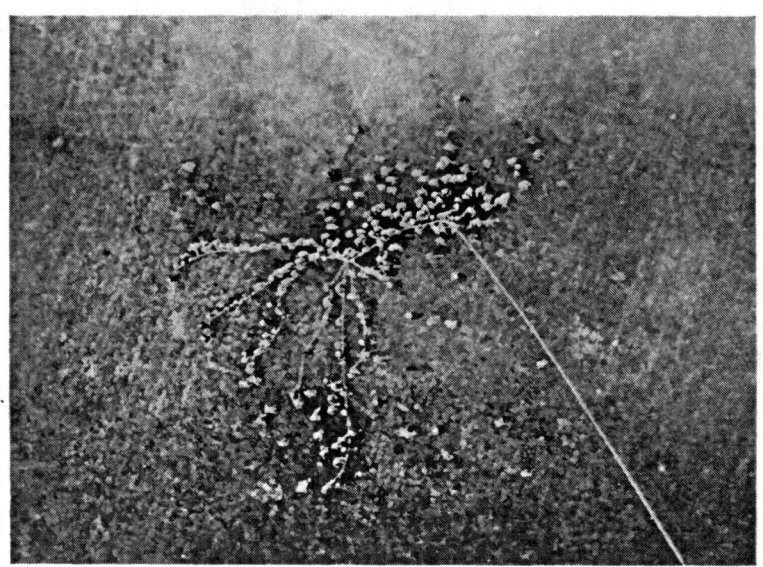

HAULING ON THE TRAIL ROPE. THE END OF THE JOURNEY.

PREPARING TO LAND AT H.M. AIRSHIP STATION, PULHAM, NORFOLK.

HOMEWARD JOURNEY 129

Secretary of State for Air : " I send my heartiest congratulations to you and to the crew of R 34 on your magnificent achievement of being the first to cross and re-cross the Atlantic by air. We are all very proud of you."

5.15 *a.m.*—From Prime Minister to General Maitland, Major Scott and the crew of H.M.A. R 34 : " Heartiest congratulations on fine feat of airmanship.—LLOYD GEORGE."

5.30 *a.m.*—We send message to Pulham as follows—

" R 34 is carrying mails, including letters for His Majesty the King. May an officer please be told off to act as special messenger and take mails immediately on ship landing."

Further wireless messages are also received from Mr. Winston Churchill, Secretary of State for War and Air, Mr. Walter Long, First Lord of the Admiralty, Admiral Sir Rosslyn Wemyss, First Sea Lord, Major-General Sir F. H. Sykes, Controller-General of Civil Aviation, and many others.

6.20 *a.m.*—Over Pulham. Quite a number of people on the landing ground despite the early hour. Scott makes two circles of the ground, and puts the ship gently down into the hands of the landing-party. Time of landing, 6.57 a.m. Total time of return journey from Long Island, New York, to Pulham, Norfolk, is therefore 75 hours and 3 minutes; or 3 days, 3 hours and 3 minutes.

APPENDICES

GROUP OF OFFICERS TAKEN AFTER LANDING.

APPENDIX I

CREW OF R 34

Officers.	Duties.
Major G. H. Scott, A.F.C.	Captain of Ship.
Captain G. S. Greenland.	Second Officer.
2nd Lieut. H. F. Luck	Third Officer.
2nd Lieut. J. D. Shotter	Engineer Officer.
Major G. G. H. Cooke, D.S.C.	Navigator.
Major J. E. M. Pritchard, O.B.E.	Special Duties.[1]
Lieut. Guy Harris	Meteorological Officer.
2nd Lieut. R. F. Durrant	Wireless Officer.
Lt.-Com. Z. Lansdowne, U.S. Navy	Representative of U.S. Naval Airship Service.[2]
Lt.-Col. W. N. Hensley.	Representative of United States Army Aviation Department.[3]
Brig.-Gen. E. M. Maitland, C.M.G., D.S.O.	Special Duties.

Other Ranks.	Duties.
S.M.2 Mayes, W. R.	First Coxswain.
Flt.-Sergt. Robinson, W. J.	Second Coxswain.
Sergt. Watson, H. M.	Riggers.
Corpl. Burgess, R. J.	
Corpl. Smith, F.	
L.A.C. Forteath, J. N.	
L.A.C. Browdie, E. P.	

[1] Major Pritchard, in addition to his other duties, was responsible for the photographic work on board, and I am indebted to him for all the illustrations.

[2] Outward journey only.

[3] Homeward journey only.

APPENDIX I

Corpl. Powell, H. R.
A.C.1 Edwards, W. J.[1]
} Wireless Telegraphy.

Flt.-Sergt. Gent, W. R.
Flt.-Sergt. Scull, N. A.
Flt.-Sergt. Ripley, R. W.
Sergt. Evenden, A. G.
Sergt. Thirlwall, J.
Corp. Cross, E. P.
L.A.C. Graham, G.
Corpl. Gray, J. H.
A.C.2 Parker, R.
A.C.2 Northeast, J.
L.A.C. Mort, J. S.
Flt.-Sergt. Turner, E. E.[1]
Flt.-Sergt. Angus, W.[1]
} Engineers.

In addition to the above, A.C.2 Ballantyne, W. W., was on board without permission, as a "stowaway," on the outward voyage.

[1] Homeward journey only.

APPENDIX II

H.M.A. R 34, WATCH AND STATION BILL.

Name.	Watch.	Landing Stations.	Flying Stations.	Mooring Stations.	Care and Maintenance.	Parachutes. On Watch.	Parachutes. Off Watch.	Parachutes. Hammock.	Prepare for Flight
W.O.2 Mayes, W. R.	Port.	Height coxswain.	Height coxswain, keel as requisite.	Height coxswain.	General supervision.	3.30–20	18	5	Secure ship, general supervision.
Sgt. Robinson, W. J.	Starboard.	Keel in charge.	Height coxswain, keel as requisite.	Keel in charge.	Keel and controls.	3.30–20	18	5	Report controls correct before and after flight.
Sgt. Watson, H. M.	Port.	Steering coxswain.	Steering coxswain, relieve height coxswain as requisite.	Steering coxswain.	Gas valves, purities and top of ship.	6.18	29	16	Before flight, top of ship, top gas valves and bumping bags, forward car. After flight, top gas valves, forward car ballast.
Cpl. Burgess, R. J.	Starboard.	Stand-by after handling guys, emergency water ballast in charge.	Keel, relieve steering or height coxswain as requisite.	After and keel as required.	Planes, wiring and handling guys.	6.18	29	16	Handling guys and tackle aft of after car before and after flight.

Name	Side	Duty 1	Duty 2	Mooring platform					Remarks
Cpl. Smith, F.	Port.	Mooring platform, forward emergency water ballast and guys.	Keel, relieve steering or height coxswain as requisite.	Mooring platform.	With 2nd coxswain in keel.	6.17	30	17	In charge of tackles amidship before and after flight.
Major Pritchard, J.E.M.	Starboard.	Mooring platform, trail ropes and emergency water ballast.	Steering coxswain, relieve height coxswain as requisite.	Amidships in keel as required.	Control car.	6.17	30	17	Trail ropes, forward tackle and handling guys before and after flight.
Lieut.-Comdr. Lansdowne, Z.	Port.	Stand-by after handling guys, emergency water ballast.	Keel, relieve steering or height coxswain as requisite.	Keel as required.	Top of ship.	20.24	21	12	Top of ship and manoeuvring valves.
L.A.C. Browdie, E.P.	Port.	Frame 19, transmission of orders.	Cook and mess-deck sweeper.	Keel as required.	Keel.	3.21–20	24	15	With 2nd coxswain.
L.A.C. Forteath, J.N.	Starboard.	Top of ladder from forward car for general transmission of orders, in event of breakdown.	Keel, relieve steering as requisite.	Winch.	Forward car.	3.21–20	24	13	Amidship handling guys.

H.M.A. R 34, WATCH AND STATION BILL—*Continued*.

Name.	Watch.	Landing Stations.	Flying Stations.	Mooring Stations.	Care and Maintenance.	Parachutes. On Wtch.	Parachutes. Off Wtch.	Parachutes. Hammock.	Prepare for Flight.
Cpl. Powell, H. R.	Port.	Forward car with Aldis Lamp.	W. T. watch.	Forward car with Aldis Lamp.	In charge of all W.T. and electrical gear.	4	22	6	W. T. and electrical.
A.C.1 Edwards, W. J.	Starboard.	W. T. cabin.	W.T. watch.	W. T. cabin.	Charge of all signalling flags and W.T. cabin.	5	25	9	W. T. and electrical.
F.-Sgt. Gent, W. R.		In charge petrol in keel.	In charge petrol in keel.	In charge petrol in keel.	Supervision of "E" ratings.	19.26	27	10	As required for filling petrol, oil and water, and running engines.
F.-Sgt. Ripley, R. W.	Port.	Port wing car in charge.	Port wing car.	Port wing car.	Port wing car.	9	10	7	
F.-Sgt. Scull, N. A.	Port.	Aft car in charge.	Aft car.	Aft car.	Aft car.	13	28	13	
Sgt. Thirlwall, J.	Port.	Starboard car in charge.	Starboard car.	Starboard car.	Starboard car.	11	12	7	
Cpl. Cross, E. P.	Port.	Forward car in charge.	Forward car.	Forward car.	Forward car.	8	7.15	2	

								As required for filling petrol, oil and water, and running engines.
Cpl. Gray, J. H.	Starboard.	Starboard car.	Starboard car.	Starboard car.	Starboard car.	11	12	8
L.A.C. Graham, G.	Starboard.	Forward car.	Forward car.	Forward car.	Forward car.	8	7.15	2
L.A.C. Mort, J. S.	Starboard.	Aft car.	Aft car.	Aft car.	Aft car.	14	23	14
Sgt. Evenden, A. G.	Starboard.	Aft car.	Aft car.	Aft car.	Aft car.	13	28	
A.C.2 Parker, R.	Port.	Mess deck as requisite.	Aft car.	Keel as requisite.	Keel for petrol tanks.	14	23	14
A.C.2 Northeast, J.	Starboard.	Port wing car.	Port wing car.	Port wing car.	Port wing car.	9	10	7

APPENDIX III

FOOD SUPPLIES FOR OUTWARD AND HOMEWARD JOURNEYS

21 lbs. cooked beef.
20 lbs. stewed beef.
5 cold hams = 35 lbs.[1]
21 lbs. meat pies.
24 four-ounce bottles of Oxo.
10 three-quarter-pound tins of cocoa.
24 tins Horlick's Malted Milk (no fresh milk).
15 tins Nestle's Milk.
28 lbs. sugar.
Salt, mustard and pepper.
14 lbs. tea.
56 lbs. potatoes, cooked in their skins.
14 two-pound tins assorted jams.
75 loaves ordinary bread.
24 loaves Veda bread, which keeps moist for quite a week.
45 lbs. cheese (Cheddar).
8 boxes of toffee (2 oz. ration per man per day).
$36\frac{1}{2}$ lbs. chocolate (4 oz. per man per day).
24 lbs. margarine.
30 eggs, all hard boiled.
45 one-pound boxes Fruitarian cake.
Three days Emergency Rations.
Bovril—mixture of chocolate, Bovril, milk and fat.
80 galls. drinking water.

[1] One ham for breakfast each day for crew of thirty. All meat cooked before starting—no tinned meat and no fresh meat.

APPENDIX III

Drinking water also in one ballast bag, weight one ton.

Total weight, 545¼ lbs.

On return journey this list was increased by—

Pickles—twelve bottles at 2 lbs.; tinned fruit—forty-eight tins at 1 lb.; and rum—twelve 1¼-pint bottles.

Other luxuries were surreptitiously stowed on board in dark by well-wishers, viz. honey, jams, candies, etc.

Altogether return journey, from a food and drink point of view, was decidedly pleasanter than outward one!

HOURS OF MEALS.

Breakfast.

7.30 a.m.	Watch going on.
8 a.m.	,, coming off.

Lunch.

11.30 a.m.	Watch going on.
12 a.m.	,, coming off.

Tea.

3.30 p.m.	Watch going on.
4 p.m.	,, coming off.

Dinner.

7.30 p.m.	Watch going on.
8 p.m.	,, coming off.

APPENDIX IV

NAVIGATIONAL INSTRUMENTS AND BOOKS USED IN R 34

Two sextants, one in forward car, and one on roof of ship.
Bubble sextant.
Battenberg—special type Mark I. for Aircraft.
Beck's bomb sight for measuring ground speed and also drift.
Open drift sight with ground speed scale.
One aircraft compass in fore car, America type.
One standard compass on top of hull.
Three chronometer watches.
One hack or deck watch.
Star globe.
Inman's Nautical Tables.
Birdwood and Davis' True Bearing Tables.
Nautical Almanac.
Newfoundland and Labrador Pilot, Vols. I. and II.
United States Pilot, East Coast. Vols. I. and II.
Nova Scotia and Bay of Fundy Pilot.
St. Lawrence Pilot. Vols. I. and II.
Admiralty List of Lights and Time Signals. Vols. I, II, IV, VI, and VIII.
Danger Angle and Off-Shore Distance Tables.
Davis' Star Azimuth Tables.
Davis' Supplementary Azimuths.
Sun's True Bearing and Azimuth Tables.
Dip and Distance Horizon Tables.
Marconi Communication Charts.
Holmes Lights for use as flares by night.
One set of Atlantic Charts, also of British Isles and N. America.

In addition we carried the following meteorological works—
Claydon, on *Cloud Studies*.
Seaman's Handbook of Meteorology.
Meteorological Glossary.

APPENDIX V

WIRELESS RESULTS ON TRANSATLANTIC FLIGHTS OF H.M.A. R 34

It is estimated that during the outward and homeward voyages, 20,000 words were sent and received by wireless, and the following notes may be of interest.

Outward Journey.
Read by H.M.S. *Queen Elizabeth* up to 1300 miles.
Read by Wormwood Scrubbs, 1100 miles.
Inter-communication established with East Fortune R.A.F. Station up to 1000 miles. East Fortune was the last and first Air Station to hold direct communication, and R 34 was in touch with Pembroke Naval Station, Ponta del Garda and St. John's, Newfoundland, during the entire voyage.

Clifden was read both ways, true note at 2000 miles.

Glace Bay was not so strong, and signals were exchanged at 1000 miles with Bar Harbour, Maine.

Marked direction effect was noticed with the ship's head to the transmitting station; that is to say, Clifden was stronger coming back at 1000 miles than at the same distance on the outward journey.

WIRELESS LOG OF H.M.A. R 34 ON TRANSATLANTIC FLIGHT

Outward Journey.
July 2nd, 1919. G.M.T. throughout.
A.M.
1.42. Left ground.
2.2. To East Fortune from R 34 : " All O.K."

APPENDIX V

A.M.
- 2.10. To R 34 from Air Ministry: "General Maitland, officers and crew of R 34. All success to your flight and good luck to all on board.—R. M. GROVES."
- 2.17. To R 34 from H.M.S. *Furious*: "All good wishes from Captain and Flying Squadron."
- 3.8. Quiet on 1400 metres.
- 3.12. From East Fortune: "Have you anything to communicate?"
- 3.14. From R 34: "Nothing to communicate."
- 3.26. From Air Ministry: "Did you listen for Clifden at 03.00?"
- 3.28. From R 34: "In accordance with rules am not starting on routine until out of touch with East Fortune."
- 3.35. From Air Ministry: "Start routine at once."
- 3.40. From R 34: "Will start routine at once."
- 3.45. To East Fortune: "Am going over to routine now."
- 4.5. Quiet—slight X's.
- 4.16. From East Fortune: "Have you anything to communicate?"
- 4.17. From R 34: "R. 20 am using type 15 with small generator, radiation 2 amps."
- 4.38. Forward engine stopped.
- 4.40. To East Fortune: "Over Rathlin."
- 4.50. Message passed by *Furious*.
- 4.52. To East Fortune: "Off Rathlin Island, North-East Ireland. 4.50 G.M.T. Steering west—going well.—SCOTT, R 34."
- 5.43. X's at intervals.
- 5.58. Faint stations calling us R. 2.
- 5.59. From R 34 K.
- 6.0. No reply.

APPENDIX V

A.M.
- 6.1. From Clifden nil.
- 6.15. Exchanging operating signals with Dundee and Air Ministry.
- 6.55. From Air Ministry: " Code weather report will be sent by Clifden at 07.00."
- 7.00. Code weather from Clifden.
- 7.48. From Ponta del Garda: H.M.S. *Tiger*: " Lat. 56.15 N., Long. 36.20 W., Bar. 30.33, falling slowly. Wind S.S.W., under 5 m.p.h. Thick fog-bank. Visibility nil. Sea moderate. 02.00."
- 7.55. Weather from Ponta.
- 8.10. From Air Ministry: " What is your position?"
- 8.23. " Position 55.20 N., 10.40 W. Course west, 40 knots. 08.20."
- 9.00. Clifden nil.
- 9.10. Clifden sent to R 34 from *Tiger*: " Position 56.15 N., 36.20 W., Bar. 30.33, falling slowly. Wind S.S.W., under 5 m.p.h. Thick fog-bank. Visibility five miles. Sea moderate."
  From *Furious*: " 05.00, Position 60 N., 25 W., Bar. 1027.5 millibars, falling slowly. Wind N.W. force 2 overcast. Visibility four miles. 08.40."
- 10.7. To East Fortune: " Going through thick fog. Everything well.—SCOTT."
- 10.50. Jamming on 1400 by local spark vessels.
- 11.00. Clifden nil.
- 11.14. Heard S.V.E. calling J.A.P.
- 11.17. G.C.K. calling Z.B.E.
- 11.22. From East Fortune: " Your signals strength 7."
- 11.45. Weather from Ponta.

P.M.
- 12.2. R 34 to *Renown*: " Pass to Air Ministry R. 1132 from B.W.P."

APPENDIX V

P.M.
- 12.5. From Scillies to R 34 : " Can you hear me ? "
- 12.7. " Yes, strength 9."
- 12.23. From Air Ministry : " What is your position ? "
- 12.27. " Position at 12.00 : 55.07 N., 14.50 W. Course 270 true. Speed 32 knots. Thick fog. All's well. 12.25."
- 12.40. On 60 metres.
- 1.00. Back on 1400 metres.
- 1.25. Gave midday position to *Renown*.
- 2.15. Exchanging strengths with East Fortune.
- 3.00. Nil from Clifden.
- 3.48. Weather from Ponta.
- 3.50. In touch with St. John's.
- 3.55. From St. John's : " Your signals are 4."
- 3.58. To St. John's.
- 4.00. Weather from St. John's.
- 4.18. From *Queen Elizabeth* : " Can you hear me ? "
- 4.20. " Yes, R 10."
- 4.22. Gave position.
- 4.35. To Air Ministry via *Queen Elizabeth* : " Position 16.30, 53.50 N., 18.00 W. All's well. 16.35."
- 5.00. Weather from Clifden.
  To Commander Lansdowne : " Would you wireless one or two messages to *New York Times* ? Address London correspondent *New York Times*." Reply few words giving impressions of voyage so far and weather.—from " International News Service."
- 5.30. Testing with St. John's.
- 6.10. To Air Ministry : " Position at 18.00, 53.20 N., 20.00 W., steaming 30 knots. 2000 feet."
- 6.20. Strengths exchanged with *Renown*.
- 6.22. To East Fortune : " Your strength R. 7."
- 6.23. From East Fortune : " Are you getting enough weather reports ? "

APPENDIX V 147

P.M.
- 6.24. " Yes. We are in touch with Pembroke, St. John's, Ponta and Clifden."
- 6.38. Called C.Q. on spark.
- 6.40. Got G.B.R.K.
- 6.42. "Hear British Airship R 34 from Scotland bound New York."
- 6.45. " Good, good, old man." Hear s.s. *Ballygally Head.* Bound Montreal from Belfast.
- 6.51. " O.K. O.M. T.K.S."—Our position given.
- 7.00. From Clifden: " Are you in communication with *Tiger* and *Renown*? "
- 7.20. To Air Ministry via *Renown*: " Yes, receiving from *Tiger.*"
- 8.20. In touch with Pembroke.
- 9.00. From Clifden: " Report at noon-to-morrow, fuel expended."
- 9.16. Still in touch with East Fortune.
- 9.30. Weather from *Renown*.
- 10.10. Ditto.
- 10.45. Weather from St. John's.
- 11.00. Clifden nil.
- 11.45. Weather from Ponta and Pembroke.

July 3rd, 1919

A.M.
- 12.17. Weather from St. John's.
- 1.35. Call to Barrington Passage.
- 1.40. No reply from Barrington. Called *Tiger*.
- 1.45. *Tiger* takes message from Air Ministry.
- 2.15. From *Tiger :* " Wait, strong X's."
- 2.56. Last heard of R 34 by East Fortune.
- 3.00. " What is your position ? " (from Clifden).
- 3.45. Weather from Ponta and position to Air Ministry at 3 a.m., 52.50 N., 28.10 W.

APPENDIX V

A.M.
- 4.10. Weather from St. John's.
- 5.00. Clifden weather.
- 5.9. *Queen Elizabeth* read us R 3.
- 5.15. Tried to D.F. on *Tiger*.
- 5.25. Called C.Q. on spark.
- 5.27. Got O.Z.B.
- 5.28. "Hear British Airship R 34."
- 5.30. "O.K. O.M. Good luck." Hear s.s. *Hellig Olav*, bound Copenhagen: "Position 28° 10′ W., 53° 10′ N."
- 6.8. To Air Ministry via St. John's: "Position at 06.00, 52° 30′ N., 30° 00′ W. 06.10."
- 7.00. Clifden nil.
- 7.25. From *Tiger* : "Position, please."
- 7.30. Repeated 06.10 position (read by *Queen Elizabeth*).
- 7.50. Weather from Ponta.
- 8.10. From St. John's: "Your strength R. 7."
- 9.00. From Clifden: "Am requesting Glace Bay to pass all messages to you from us thirty minutes past odd hours."
- 9.30. Curious static charging receiver between cloud layers 2000 to 4000 feet.
- 9.45. Tuning for Glace Bay. Capacity added stops X's, heard Glace Bay for first time. R. 6.
- 9.50. Call Barrington Passage. No reply.
- 10.15. *Tiger* calling Barrington Passage. No reply.
- 10.55. Call Barrington.
- 11.00. Clifden weather.
- 11.10. To Air Ministry via *Tiger* : "Position at 09.00, 34° 30′ W., 52° 50′ N."

P.M.
- 12.3. Weather from St. John's.
- 1.00. From Clifden: "Position, please."
- 1.35. Heard *Aquitania* R. 5.

APPENDIX V 149

P.M.
- 1.37. To Air Ministry via *Tiger:* " Position 12.00, 52° 30′ N., 37° 00′ W. 1546 gallons of fuel expended. 13.45."
- 2.5. Passed messages to St. John's for *Tiger*.
- 2.50. Hauled aerial in for temperature to be taken, can see waves.
- 3.10. Bright sunlight.
- 3.40. Called C.Q. spark.
- 3.42. Hear s.s. *Canada* bound Liverpool: " Position 51° 16′ N., 39° 42′ W. Moderate S.E. wind and sea. Weather clear. Bar. 30.08, rising.—DAVIS."
- 3.56. " Thanks." Passed to Air Ministry: " Position 10° N., 40° 30′ W. Petrol expended, 1546 gallons; fuel left, 3354 gallons."
- 4.30. Weather from St. John's.
- 5.00. Clifden weather.
- 6.30. Position to *Tiger :* " 52° 25′ N., 40° 40′ W."
- 6.52. To St. John's for Clements Met. Officer : " Position 52° 25′ N., 42° 35′ W. Wind S.E.E. 45 knots. at 800 feet. Proposed going north of centre. Please forward any information.—Lt. GUY HARRIS, R 34."
- 7.00. Clifden weather.
- 7.45. Azores weather.
- 7.50. Pembroke weather.
- 8.18. St. John's weather.
- 8.27. To St. John's: " Inform Admiral Mark Kerr, Handley-Page Aerodrome, that General Maitland is aboard."
- 8.30. Spoke s.s. *Megantic*.
- 8.55. From *Tiger*, weather.
- 10.00. X's bad.
- 10.30. X's still strong.
- 11.00. Clifden weather.
- 11.45. Azores weather.

APPENDIX V

July 4th, 1919

A.M.

12.29. From St. John's: "Handley-Page probably leaving for New York at 10.30 a.m. to-day."
12.45. To *Megantic:* "Is there D.F. Station at Cape Race?"
12.47. "Yes, D.F. at Cape Race. Call V.C.E."
12.50. Called V.C.E.
12.52. From *Megantic* to Cape Race: "Airship R 34 is calling you. Can you hear him?"
12.55. From Cape Race to all ships: "Urgent. Stop transmitting. Government message."
1.00. No luck with Cape Race. Over 300 miles from him.
1.47. First report from Barrington Passage. X's bad.
2.7. *Tiger* weather.
3.00. From Clifden: "Inform Air Ministry immediately you sight St. John's."
3.30. Glace Bay repeated above.
4.00. To St. John's: "Position at 03.00, 51° 20' N., 48° 30' W."
5.00. X's very bad. Phones burn out. Rigged up new pair.
6.00. Cannot read through X's.
7.10. Weather from *Tiger.*
7.20. To *Tiger:* "Position 48.40 N., 49.30 W."
8.37. From *Megantic:* "Position at midnight, 49° 48' N., 42° 23' W."
9.10. Got Cape Race (250 miles).
9.15. Sending V's for bearing.
9.20. From Cape Race: "Your bearing at 9.15 a.m., 36 degrees E. of true N."
9.22. From R 34: "Thanks very much."
9.30. From Cape Race: "I have radios for you."
9.32. "Go ahead."

APPENDIX V

A.M.
- 9.35. To R 34 from Canadian Pacific Railway: "Hearty greetings to the crew R 34 on its initial trip across the Atlantic. Can you give us any story, please?—MCMILLAN, Manager of Telegraphs."
- 10.21. To Toronto Weather Bureau: "Full reports requested of American coast."
- 10.40. Above sent to U.S. Weather Bureau.
- 11.45. Weather from Barrington Passage.

P.M.
- 12.15. To Air Ministry via Barrington Passage: "Position at noon 49° 05' N., 50° 25 'W.—clear sky—low fog."
- 12.18. From St. John's to General Maitland, officers and crew: "On behalf of Newfoundland I greet you as you pass on your enterprising journey.—HARRIS, Governor."
- 12.25. To Governor of Newfoundland: "Major Scott, officers and crew R 34 send grateful thanks for kind message, with which I beg to associate myself.—GENERAL MAITLAND."
- 12.35. To R 34 from S.N.O., St. John's: "Request to be informed if you intend passing over St. John's, and if so, what time?"
- 12.37. "Yes, probably about 4 p.m. G.M.T."
- 1.5. From Clifden: "Report fuel expended and number of engines in use."
- 1.20. To Air Ministry via St. John's: "Expended 2900 gallons of petrol. All engines running well. Position 49° 05' N., 50° 20' W. 13.17."
- 1.30. Hear G.B. R. 6.—Clifden R. 5.
- 1.58. V's to V.A.Z. (Canso) for bearing.
- 2.00. From Canso repeat jammed.
- 2.5. Another radio for Commander Lansdowne from Cape Race.
- 2.45. To C.C.6: "What is your highest spark wave? I

APPENDIX V

P.M.

        want to D.F. you on 2500 metres. Can you reach it?"

2.52. C.C.6 on 2000 spark.

2.57. From C.C.6: "Send V's. I will D.F. you."

2.59. R 34 sending V's to C.C.6.

4.00. From St. John's: "Local authorities informed of your position and intention of passing over St. John's. Can we be of any assistance? Congratulations on successful voyage. Martynside aeroplane will attempt to join you."

4.10. To St. John's: "Tell Mr. Raynham to beware of long aerials hanging from R 34 when he gets near us."

4.15. To St. John's: "Have sighted land through gap in clouds, not sure of position. What is cloud height?"

4.22. From St. John's: "Clouds about 2000–3000 feet."

5.00. First land seen from cabin window.

5.34. Curious effect of signals dying away and gradually becoming stronger (due to hills).

5.43. From C.C.6: "My position Lat. 48°44′, Long. 53°40′ W. at 16.09. Your true bearing 15 or 195 degrees. 17.35."

5.50. Very long weather report from Barrington Passage.

6.10. Called Barrington.—No reply.

6.40. From Cape Race: "Radio No. 1, please state time of landing at New York.—LUCAS."

6.45. Via Cape Race to Lucas, New York: "Landing early Sunday morning.—SCOTT, R 34."

7.00. Weather from St. John's.

7.30. Ditto.

7.45. From Glace Bay—from General Seely: "Warmest congratulation to General Maitland and to all your gallant comrades. Best wishes for completion of voyage."

APPENDIX V

P.M.
8.00. Air Ministry: " Position at 20.00, 45° 56′ N., 56° 14′ W. Course W., 45 knots. All well."
8.30. Spoke s.s. *Metagama:* " Hearty congratulations—your progress watched with much interest. All success.—MILLER."
8.50. From R 34 : "Position 8.48 100 miles E.N.E. Cape Breton. Thanks for wishes.—Commander R 34."
9.4. Spoke s.s. *Seal*—bound Australia.
9.7. From *Seal:* " Good luck. God speed."
9.50. Weather from Barrington Passage.
10.18. Weather from United States Bureau.
11.00. Cape Race in touch with Handley-Page.
11.5. Intercepted from Cape Race to Handley-Page : " Dempsey knocked Willard out in third round."
11.20. From Canso : " Your bearing from us 62 degrees E. of true north."
11.25. From Cape Race to Handley-Page : " How are you going on ? Send V's for bearing."
11.28. From Handley-Page to Cape Race : " Going strong, 85 m.p.h."
11.45. Weather from St. John's.
11.52. To R 34 : " Hear Handley-Page; is that the Atlantic Airship? "
11.55. " Yes. O.M. Bound New York."
11.58. H.-P. signals.—Break off suddenly (approximate time of crash).

July 5th.
A.M.
1.00. Getting spark set accurately tuned with V.C.O.
1.30. Weather from Glace Bay. Atmospherics very strong.
2.15. Atmospherics terrific, but watch still kept.
2.30. Barrington weather report.
2.45. From Canso : " Where are you now ? "

x

APPENDIX V

A.M.
- 2.47. From R 34 to Canso: "Making towards New York."
- 2.48. From Canso: "Do you want bearing?"
- 2.52. "Not yet. O.M."
- 2.53. "Righto, any time."
- 3.30. Glace Bay repeats General Seeley's message.
- 3.55. From Barrington Passage: "I have 700 words weather for you. Can I carry on or send it at intervals?"
- 4.00. From R 34: "Go right ahead."
- 5.00. Receiving 700 words weather from Barrington.
- 5.58. From R 34: "At 1500 feet. Hope to reach Halifax by dawn."
- 6.15. From Canso: "Your bearing 81 E. of us. Handley-Page has crashed."
- 6.18. From R 34: "Anyone hurt in H.-P.?"
- 6.20. "No news yet. O.M."
- 6.23. Tried telephony with Canso.
- 6.28. From Canso: "Good. Speech fine. That's the stuff to give 'em."
- 7.15. From Canso: "Are you on the sea side or land side of us?"
- 7.20. From R 34: "On sea side of you."
- 7.45. Weather from Barrington.
- 7.50. From R 34 to Barrington: "Have passed over coast north of Trinity Bay; am proceeding to New York, passing out over Fortune Bay."
- 8.25. From Canso: "Have you anything for me or Navy, Halifax?"
- 8.29. From R 34: "Wait."
- 8.52. To Canso to Navy, Halifax: "Meeting stormy headwind. If required could you supply destroyer to tow, please?—08.50.—SCOTT, Commander, R 34."

APPENDIX V

A.M.
- 8.55. Canso passing 08.50 to Halifax.
- 9.15. From R 34 to Canso: "Have you reply from Halifax?"
- 9.17. "Not yet. You are just going out of sight of us."
- 9.22. Canso: "Request weather from St. John's, New Brunswick."
- 9.25. From Canso: "Will relay it on. It will have to go through three stations."
- 10.00. From R 34: "Hurry weather and Halifax replies."
- 10.5. From Canso: "Doing my best. O.M."
- 10.55. R 34 sending V's for position.
- 11.5. From Canso: "Your bearing at 11.00, 245 Canso, 60 from Chebucto."
- 11.15. From Halifax: "No destroyers available, only tugs here."
- 11.20. From Canso: "Weather at St. John's, N.B., wind S.W. Clear sky, clouds low."

P.M.
- 1.5. To Air Ministry via Barrington Passage: "Flying across Nova Scotia. Stormy headwind. Petrol beginning to get short. 13.00."
- 2.00. Atmospherics now terrific. Got shock through headphones, and drew sparks off aerial.
- 2.30. Second pair of phones burnt out. X's very strong.
- 2.40. Got in touch with Bar Harbour.
- 2.42. From Bar Harbour: "Can you send on C.W.? I will send C.W., 1900 metres."
- 2.43. From R 34: "Yes. Will use 1400 meters."
- 2.45. Weather from Bar Harbour.
- 3.00. From R 34 to Bar Harbour: "To Operations (Aviation) Navy Department, Washington, D.C., and to Commander, 2nd Naval District, Boston, Mass.: Could destroyers proceed if required to southern end Bay of Fundy and take H.M.A.

APPENDIX V

P.M.

      R 34 in tow? Signed Lansdowne for Captain, R 34."

3.45. To R 34 from U.S. Navy: "Arrangements have been made for destroyers to be south of Cape Cod. Arrangements are being made to temporarily land you at Montauk if it becomes essential."

3.56. Weather from Bar Harbour: "Showers and local thunderstorms probably late to-night and Sunday along the coast."

4.00. To R 34: "Destroyers *Bancroft* and *Stevens* left Boston to your assistance at 3.30 p.m.—Signed, Commander 1st Naval District."

5.00. From O.U.8: "Can I help?"

5.15. From O.U.8: "French sloop *Somme* proceeding now to southern end of Bay of Fundy. She will get there quicker than we can."

5.35. From R 34: "We are proceeding down Bay of Fundy."

5.40. From R 34 to Navy Department, Washington: "Position of R 34 noon 75th Meridian time—Lat. 45° 20′ N., Long. 64° W. Course S.W. true. Speed 20 knots. Steaming down coast of New Brunswick and Maine. Petrol running short. Please have destroyer meet us early as possible.—Signed, LANSDOWNE, for Captain, R 34."

5.48. Bar Harbour giving above message to destroyer, prefixed "Rush."

6.15. Atmospherics very bad.

7.15. Atmospherics getting worse. Tried one valve on T.F.

8.00. Atmospherics render reading impossible.

8.30. Ditto.

9.00. Hauled in aerial, approaching storm.

9.15. Ship swaying badly.

9.20. Tried to let aerial out again, but it charged up quickly.

APPENDIX V

P.M.
- 9.30. Ship caught edge of storm.
- 10.30. Aerial out again.
- 10.35. In touch with U.S. destroyers.
- 10.36. From destroyer *Bancroft*: " Course for Chatham; will make flare."
- 10.50. Flares seen. Shone Aldis Lamp down.
- 10.55. From destroyer : " You are directly above us."
- 10.58. O.K.

July 6th.

A.M.
- 12.10. From R 34 to C.O., U.S.N.A., Chatham, Mass.: " If through shortage gasolene R 34 wishes to land Chatham, can you supply 50,000 cubic feet hydrogen and 500 gallons gasolene ?—LANSDOWNE, for Captain, R 34."
- 1.30. From destroyer : " Are you heading for Chatham ? "
- 1.40. From R 34 : " Yes. Course 2.30 true. Speed 23 knots."
- 2.00. C.O., U.S.N.A.S., Montauk, Long Island : " Can you land R 34 and give us 300 gallons gasolene ? will arrive over Montauk 8 o'clock this morning.—LANSDOWNE."
- 2.50. From Navy, Washington : " Advise 1st District immediately if you can land Montauk. If you can facilities for landing have been provided."
- 3.00. From destroyer : " Will make flares again."
- 3.10. From R 34 : " You are still beneath us."
- 4.00. From Navy, Washington : " Personnel and material waiting at Mineola for instructions from you. Advise if you desire base elsewhere. Keep me informed of your movements.—LUCAS."
- 4.15. To U.S. Navy : " Will land Montauk. Will report time later."

APPENDIX V

A.M.
- 4.18. From destroyer: "Was our last rocket ahead or astern of you?"
- 4.19. From R 34: "Astern."
- 5.30. From destroyer: "Have you sighted Chatham?"
- 5.35. From R 34: "Not yet."
- 6.30. Atmospherics start again.
- 7.00. From Navy, Washington: "Arrangements being made to temporarily land ship Montauk if it becomes essential. Advise landing Mineola. Keep us informed."
- 8.00. Heavy jamming on 600 meters.
- 9.30. From R 34 to Navy, Washington: "Will land Montauk and take in petrol."
- 9.40. From R 34: "Weather over Long Island, please."
- 9.50. From R 34: "If when we reach Montauk we decide to go on, can we reach Hazelhurst Fields?"
- 10.00. To R 34: "Here *City of Augusta* bound Boston. You are over Block Island."
- 10.5. From R 34: "Keep out. You are interfering."
- 10.15. From New York: "The American Flying Club cordially invite as guests of the A.F.C. the crew of R 34 during their stay in New York at the Hotel Commodore."
- 11.45. To Hazelhurst Field: "Have passed Montauk; making a dash for Hazelhurst Field—expect to land 2 p.m. G.M.T."
- 11.48. To base: "Landing at 1 p.m. G.M.T., not 2 p.m. Barometer and temperature, please."

P.M.
- 12.5. From base: "Pressure 2979. Temperature, 80 degrees."
- 12.30. Telephony with base.
- 1.00. From base: "Lieutenant Hoyt, U.S.N., is on

APPENDIX V 159

P.M.

landing-ground ready to land you. Major Fuller not here yet."

1.35. Landed.

(Sgd.) R. F. DURRANT, 2nd Lieut.,
Wireless Officer, R 34.

WIRELESS LOG OF R 34, RETURN JOURNEY—
NEW YORK TO ENGLAND

July 10th, 1919.

A.M.

3.55. Left ground.

Let 50 feet of aerial out at 1000 feet. Good signals.
4.20. Over New York.
4.50. Still over New York. Battleships signalling to each other.
5.4. New York calling us.
5.14. From R 34: "Using low power and small aerial while over city."
5.24. Very long weather report from ships via New York.
6.30. From New York: "Can you use C.W.?"
6.35. On C.W. 1400 meters.
7.00. More weather from New York.
7.8. From New York to Dirigible R 34: "Thanks for the flight, from thousands whom the spectacle thrilled. Good luck to you.—*New York Times*."
7.15. From New York: "God speed you on return to England. Hope your voyage is only forerunner of many.—*New York Herald*."
7.20. To Air Attaché, Air Ministry and base, via New York: "Course 90° true, speed 50 knots, going well."
7.25. From New York W.T.: "Good luck to you."
7.30. Atmospherics getting strong.
7.45. Now getting all weather from Bar Harbour.

APPENDIX V

A.M.
9.00.
P.M.
3.00. } Fifteen weather reports from Bar Harbour.

3.5. Started routine.
3.10. Weather report from Barrington Passage.
3.14. To Air Ministry via Barrington: " Position at 16.00, Long. 60° 50′ W., Lat. 42° 00′ N. 60 knots. All's well."
5.5. To U.S. Weather Bureau: " Many thanks for kind, efficient manner in which weather information has been supplied; deeply grateful.—GUY HARRIS, Met. Officer, R 34."
5.20. Weather from Bar Harbour.
6.44. Ditto.
7.00. Atmospherics very strong.
8.20. Phones burnt out.
9.00. Using American phones.
9.34. To Bar Harbour: " Position at 8.50 p.m., 42° 15′ N., 54° 05′ W. Course E., 50 knots."
10.55. H.M.S. *Tiger* heard R 2 X's.
11.00. From Clifden nil.
11.30. From Glace Bay—from Air Ministry: " Position at 16.00 received. Report fuel consumed."
11.56. Called C.Q. on spark.
11.58. Here British ship *Minnekahda* bound Halifax with troops. " I am in touch with Cape Race."
12.00. " Thanks."

July 11*th.*

A.M.
12.5. From Bar Harbour: " Do you want last night's Press ? "
12.7. " No, thanks."
12.15. From Bar Harbour: " I will keep continuous watch on 1400 after you lose me."

APPENDIX V

A.M.
- 12.17. " Thanks, O.M."
- 1.20. Weather from Bar Harbour.
- 1.50. From Barrington: " Disturbance over Newfoundland. Barometer 29.52, moving north, likely to disappear."
- 2.17. Weather from Bar Harbour.
- 3.20. " In touch with Sable Island. All's well."
- 3.30. Via Bar Harbour to Admiral Commanding Naval District, Mineola: " Officers and crew R 34 desire to express their sincere gratitude for the valuable and efficient assistance they have received during the mooring out of R 34 at Mineola. All well. Making good progress. Distance covered, 630 miles in twelve hours. Making for London.—SCOTT."
- 4.00. Via Bar Harbour to Colonel Miller, Long Island: " Officers and crew R 34 thank you personally for trouble you have taken to help us while moored out. It is much appreciated. Going strong for London. Distance covered in twelve hours, 630 miles.—SCOTT."
- 4.20. Atmospherics very bad.
- 4.50. From Clifden—from Air Ministry: " Indicate position through Ponta Del Garda, immediately communication is established."
- 4.56. Via Ponta: " Static fierce. Long distance communication will be O.K. by daylight.—Signed, DURRANT."
- 5.0. Atmospherics still very strong.
- 5.2. To Ponta for Air Ministry: " Position at 04.00, Lat. 43° 40′ N., Long. 46° 00′ W. Course 72 degrees true. Speed 45 knots."
- 5.10. From Clifden nil.
- 7.00. Clifden jammed by small boat underneath saying: " You are on our port bow."

APPENDIX V

A.M.
- 7.30. Weather from Ponta.
- 7.55. Weather from St. John's.
- 8.25. Weather from *Tiger*.
- 9.11. Weather from Clifden, timed, 08.30.
- 9.30. To *Tiger*: " Everything going well."
- 10.15. To Air Ministry, via *Tiger*: " Position at 10.00. Lat. 45° 30' N., Long. 40° 20' W. Speed 20 knots, 10.25."
- 10.45. Spoke s.s. *San Florino*, bound Tampico, Mexico, from Southampton.
- 11.00. From Clifden, weather.
- 11.45. Weather from Ponta.

P.M.
- 1.00. From Clifden—from Air Ministry : " Following arrangements have been made for you on arrival : Accommodation available at East Fortune and Pulham, and in emergency Kingsnorth. Airship Officer and necessary landing-party with supply of petrol is at Fermoy, 15 miles N.N.E. of Cork. Destroyers with steam at one hour's notice are at Berehaven."
- 1.30. To Air Ministry, via *Tiger*: " Position at 13.25, 13° 54' W., 46° 40' N."
- 3.00. From Clifden : " Request position."
- 3.20. From St. John's, from New York: " At this luncheon given by Aerial Club of America resolutions were passed to the effect that the Club wish General Maitland and crew of R 34 a very pleasant journey.—LUCAS."
- 4.00. Weather from Ponta.
- 5.00. Weather from Clifden.
- 6.40. In touch with H.M.S. *Cumberland*. Her position at 19.00, 50° 32' N., 35° 00' W.
- 7.45. Weather from Ponta.
- 7.50. K.A. 7 (R. 50) called Ponta.

APPENDIX V 163

P.M.
- 8.5. To Ponta, for Air Ministry: " Tell Irish D.F. Stations to look out for us."
- 9.00. Tried to D.F. *Cumberland.*
- 10.00. Heard s.s. *Orduna.*
- 10.44. Intercepted East Fortune; heard him say, " Saturday night " (1100 miles).
- 11.00. From Clifden: " All Irish D.F. stations closed."
- 11.14. Position to Air Ministry at 23.13: " 50° 16′ N., 33° 00′ W."
- 11.23. Spoke s.s. *Dominion*, bound Avonmouth.
- 11.25. From *Dominion* : " Shall I fire a gun when I think you are near me? Estimate your speed at 45 m.p.h.—CHRISTIE."
- 11.27. From R 34: " No; don't trouble to fire a gun."
- 11.48. Weather from Ponta.
- 11.56. Atmospherics getting stronger.

July 12*th.*
A.M.
- 12.53. From East Fortune: " Your signals are strength 5."
- 12.57. From R 34: Ditto.
- 1.00. From Clifden: " Weather conditions at East Fortune extremely doubtful. Steer for Pulham."
- 1.23. To Air Ministry: " Am about 1000 from you now."
- 1.39. From East Fortune: " What is your position? "
- 1.42. To East Fortune: " You are stronger than Air Ministry."
- 2.5. Position at 02.00, 51° 12′ N. Long., 30° 00′ W. Lat. Course 90. Speed 40 knots.
- 3.00. From Air Ministry: " Major Scott, R 34. Best luck. Thumbs up.—MALCOLM FRASER."
- 3.10. To R 34: " Hearty congratulations. Best luck to all on board. From Sonic Works, Constantinesco."
- 5.00. Weather from Clifden.
- 6.15. Ships jamming on 1400 meters.
- 6.37. To East Fortune: " Position at 06.30, 52° 15′ N., Course N. 70° E. true. 35 knots."

Y 2

APPENDIX V

A.M.
- 7.00. From Clifden nil.
- 7.32. Weather from *Tiger*.
- 7.46. Weather from Ponta.
- 7.48. Weather from St. John's.
- 7.57. Weather from Pembroke.
- 8.00. Working direct to East Fortune. Our signals are now strength 7 to East Fortune.
- 8.40. From East Fortune: " Weather conditions last night on ground wind nearly up and down shed, 10 to 15 m.p.h. Do not anticipate anything worse to-night. Consider it could be possible to safely house you between 21.00 and 08.00. B.S.T."
- 9.30. Weather report from East Fortune.
- 10.5. C.Q. on spark.
- 10.8. In touch with s.s. *Masirah*. Position, Lat. 53° 30′ N., Long. 18° 10′ W.
- 11.00. Weather from Clifden.
- 11.10. From Fermoy : " Do you intend to land at Fermoy, for I have landing party of 500 men if required ?— MAJOR LITTLE."
- 11.13. From R 34 : " No, not landing at Fermoy."
- 11.14. Position at 11.00, 52° 55′ N., 19° 30′ W.
- 11.33. To Air Ministry : " Request all traffic may come direct on 1400."
- 11.39. From Air Ministry : " Yes, certainly. Am instructing Clifden to stop routine."

P.M.
- 12.15. Weather from East Fortune.
- 1.30. To East Fortune : " Noon position, 53° 19′ N., 17° 23′ W."
- 2.12. Intercepted from East Fortune to T. 75 : " Drop pamphlets over coast town."
- 3.50. Bearing of Clifden on D.F. frame 150.
- 6.45. Weather from Ponta.

APPENDIX V

P.M.
- 8.00. Weather from East Fortune.
- 8.15. Passing over coast at Clifden Wireless Station.
- 8.45. To East Fortune : " Passed over Clifden, heading N. 56 E."
- 8.51. To East Fortune : " Request weather report."
- 10.00. From East Fortune : " Wind indefinite on surface. At 1500 feet between W. and N.W., 10 m.p.h. Consider conditions will be favourable for landing you at 10.00 to-morrow."
- 10.10. To Air Ministry : " East Fortune report weather conditions favourable for landing to-morrow morning. Request permission to proceed and land at East Fortune.—SCOTT, 20.10."
- 10.55. From Air Ministry : " Reference your 20.10. Land at Pulham. Acknowledge."
- 11.18. To Air Ministry—priority : " Can land at East Fortune 6 a.m. Cannot land Pulham until 10 a.m. One engine completely broken down. Others may fail at any moment. Request Air Ministry may reconsider their decision."
- 11.30. From R 34 : " Hasten reply."
- 11.55. From Air Ministry : " Proceed to Pulham. If by doing so you anticipate risk of breakdown, report to Air Ministry."

July 13th.
A.M.
- 12.27. To East Fortune : " Position 54° 30′ N., 60° 0′ W. Course S.E. 60 knots."
- 12.41. To East Fortune : " In accordance with Air Ministry instructions, I am proceeding to Pulham. Please have officers' and ratings' kit sent to Pulham as soon as possible.—MAJOR SCOTT."
- 3.00. To Pulham : " Probable time of landing, 06.00 G.M.T."
- 3.45. Weather from Air Ministry.

APPENDIX V

A.M.

4.20. From Air Ministry, from His Majesty the King: "I heartily congratulate you all on your safe return home after the completion of your memorable and indeed unique Atlantic voyage.—GEORGE, R.I."

4.40. From Air Ministry to General Maitland, Major Scott, officers and crew of R 34: "On behalf of the whole Air Force I send you heartiest congratulations on your magnificent achievement, in making the double journey across the Atlantic.—TRENCHARD, Chief of Air Staff."

4.46. From Board of Admiralty to General Maitland and crew of H.M.A. R 34: "Welcome home. The great adventure of R 34 is beyond all praise.—Board of Admiralty."

5.00. From General Seeley, Under-Secretary of State: "I send my heartiest congratulations to you and to the crew of R 34 on your magnificent achievement of being the first to cross and re-cross the Atlantic by air. We are all very proud of you."

5.15. From Prime Minister to General Maitland, Major Scott and the crew of H.M.A. R 34: "Heartiest congratulations on fine feat of airmanship.—LLOYD GEORGE."

6.30. To C.O., Pulham: "R 34 is carrying mails, including letters for His Majesty the King. May an officer, please, be told off to act as special messenger and take mails immediately on ship landing."

7.00. Aerial hauled in.

(Sgd.) R. F. DURRANT, 2nd Lieut.,
Wireless Officer, R 34.

APPENDIX VI

HANDLING SHIP DURING THE NIGHT. AEROSTATIC CONDITIONS

THE Airship left Scotland at the coolest part of the night, and almost completely full of gas. She left the ground with just sufficient buoyancy to get clear of the shed and surrounding obstructions. The engines were then started, and the ship driven to the requisite height for crossing Scotland dynamically on her engines. Owing to the foggy nature of the weather it was necessary to rise to 1500 feet, to avoid the danger of colliding with high ground in the fog. This necessitated loss of gas to the extent of over two tons lift. After sunrise the gas superheated and, although the ship was flown at about 1000 feet, a large amount of gas was unavoidably lost. After sunset this superheating effect disappeared, and the ship lost buoyancy to the extent of the gas lost soon after sunrise, due to overheating—say three tons. A further effect which caused ship to lose buoyancy was the foggy and generally low-lying nature of the clouds through which the ship had to pass about sunset. As an offset to this loss in buoyancy the ship had become lighter by the extent of the petrol consumed.

The net result of these above-mentioned losses and gains in buoyancy was about four to five tons negative buoyancy at sunset, July 2nd. This necessitated the ship being flown at an angle of about ten degrees up by the bow with all engines running at cruising speed (1600 revs.), as otherwise

APPENDIX VI

ballast in the form of petrol would have had to have been jettisoned to prevent the ship from descending into the sea.

The next morning (July 3rd)—after sunrise—the same superheating effect was experienced, but owing to the weight of petrol consumed during the night, and to the gas already lost through superheating in the morning of July 2nd, it was no longer necessary to lose gas, and the ship became light. As it was desirable to maintain the ship in this light condition to allow for the loss of superheating at sunset, she was driven down by her elevators into the fog—the top of which was about 1500 feet—in order to cool down the gas, and thus get rid of the false lift caused by superheating.

CPSIA information can be obtained at www.ICGtesting.com
Printed in the USA
BVOW05s1050270314

348964BV00010B/274/P